DK

AN ANTHOLOGY OF
Shells

WARNING NOTE FROM THE PUBLISHER: This book is an introduction to the amazing world of shells and is not a field guide for shell collection. In some countries, the collection of some or all shells is restricted or prohibited by law, so know what the rules are. Never take any shells that contain a living animal, and, even where permitted, do not take many shells from one place, as the local ecosystem often relies also on empty shells. Consider taking photos instead of taking shells. Be aware before handling that some shells can cause injury through sharp edges and even venomous stings, and remember to take an adult with you when you go looking for shells.

AN ANTHOLOGY OF
Shells

Written by Simon P. Aiken
Illustrated by Angela Rizza and Daniel Long

Contents

What are shells?...6

Where are shells found?..................................8

GASTROPODS...10

Ringed top...11

Spotted top..12

Australian pheasant shell.................................13

Girdled star shell..14

Long-spined dolphin shell.................................15

Bleeding tooth...16

Moriori abalone..17

South African keyhole limpet.............................18

Prince's horn shell.......................................19

West African mud creeper................................20

Hefty screw shell..21

Vomer conch...22

Bull conch...23

Fingered spider conch....................................24

Miraculous soft-cap......................................25

Shell collectors of the sea..............................26

Zigzag cowrie..28

Golden cowrie...29

Great spotted cowrie.....................................30

Maltese cross cowrie.....................................31

Cape cowrie..32

The Emperor's egg cowrie................................33

Blistered egg cowrie......................................34

Violet moon shell..35

Pot-bellied fig...36

Galápagos helmet shell...................................37

Musical shells...38

Winged triton..40

Neapolitan triton...41

Robinson's distortion shell................................42

Lamarck's frog shell......................................43

Splendid niso...44

Common wentletrap......................................45

Hessler's hairy vent shell.................................46

Checkerboard goblet shell................................47

Japanese corded whelk...................................48

Torr's whelk...49

Lightning whelk..50

Lined spindle shell.......................................51

Splendid dove shell......................................52

Pimpled mud shell.......................................53

Persian horse conch......................................54

Festive mini-spindle......................................55

Protected shells...56

Rose-branch murex.......................................58

Orchid murex..59

Venus comb...60

Club murex..61

Butterfly murex..62

Pavlova's typhis...63

Burnett's thorn-mouth....................................64

Spiny coral shell...65

False trumpet shell.......................................66

Zanzibar vase..67

Spiky pagoda shell.......................................68

Kuiper's ribbed miter.....................................69

Spiral Babylon	70
Onion shell	71
Festive volute	72
Ponsonby's volute	73
Clover's volute	74
Mrs. Roadnight's volute	75
Love harp	76
Queen margin shell	77
Uncoiled nutmeg	78
Cracked miter	79
Tent olive	80
False olive	81
Victor cone	82
Textile cone	83
The glory cones	84
Revolving cone	86
Wonder shell	87
Blushing auger	88
Perspective sundial	89
Red-lined bubble	90
Unbound bubble	91
Is it a shell?	92
Decorated lake snail	94
Spiny freshwater snail	95
Mrs. De Burgh's tropid snail	96
Little miracle snail	97
The hedgehog snail from hell	98
The snowflake snail	99
Liguus tree snail	100
Up-mouth snail	101
Pinched door snail	102
Green-banded snail	103
Exploding snail	104
Yellow-banded mirror snail	105
Shells for decoration	106

BIVALVES ... 108
Crowned cockle	109
Wedding cake Venus	110
Spined Venus	111
Beautiful sunset clam	112
Victoria thorny oyster	113
Somali scallop	114
Diana's scallop	115
Square window-pane clam	116
Australian watering pot	117
Elliptical African oyster	118
Pistolgrip	119

OTHER TYPES OF MOLLUSKS ... 120
Paper nautilus	121
Spectacular chiton	122
Formosan tusk	123
Glossary	124
Index	126
Acknowledgments	128

What are shells?

Perhaps you've seen them on the beach. Perhaps they are decorating your house or among the soil in your garden. Maybe you've been to a museum and seen a magnificent display of their different colors, patterns, and shapes—some shiny, some spiny, some gigantic, and others smaller than a pinhead. We are talking about shells! In this book, we'll look at mollusk shells—shells that are created by soft-bodied animals called mollusks.

Outer skeleton

You have a skeleton on your inside, but a mollusk has its skeleton on the outside. This outer skeleton, or "exoskeleton," is its shell. The mollusk pictured here is called Johnson's volute (*Lyria pauljohnsoni*). The delicate, purple-and-yellow parts of the mollusk can hide inside the shell for protection.

Large, muscular "foot"

Lime

Shells are made of chemicals similar to lime. It's the mollusk itself that creates the shell. Many shells have 3D shapes or patterns on the surface, called sculpture. For instance, this annularid land snail (*Abbottella moreletiana*) has rows of short spines on its shell.

Head

How shells are named

Experts give a name to each type of shell using the Latin language. This scientific name usually has two parts and is written in *italic* letters. The first part notes the genus of a group of shells. The second part notes the name of the particular species in that genus. For instance, this shell is *Gyroscala lamellosa*. For this book, we'll mainly use the common names.

The common name of this shell is the flaked wentletrap.

Two-piece shells

Some mollusks have a two-piece shell, like this flame shell (*Limaria hians*). Two-piece shells are called bivalves, and each half is called a "valve." The valves are hinged together so that the animal can open them to feed or clamp them shut to protect itself.

Tentacles

Upper valve

Lower valve

Where are shells found?

To learn about an animal, we need to know where it lives and how it is suited to its habitat. Shelled mollusks thrive in many different habitats. You will find them in the sea (seashells), on land, and also in lakes and rivers.

Coral reefs

The warm waters of the tropics have the biggest variety of shells, which are especially colorful. Coral reefs are made of living creatures, called corals, which some shelled mollusks eat. Sponges living in the reefs also provide food for mollusks.

Sponges are delicate animals that come in all colors.

The seashore

If you live near the sea, you've probably seen shells on the beach. But very few of the mollusks they belong to live on the sand. Instead, they might live in a rocky tidal pool, where they can find protection from crashing waves and can get plenty to eat!

Rock pools can contain amazing animals and plants.

The deep sea

Shelled mollusks also live in the deepest parts of the ocean, where there is no light. Some deep-sea mollusks are discovered when they accidentally get caught in fishing nets. Others can be seen only by very specialized submarines.

More than 40,000 species of shelled mollusks live in the ocean.

Lakes, rivers, and streams

At least 5,000 more species of shelled mollusks live in fresh water (water with no salt in it), such as rivers, streams, and lakes. Some of these mollusks live in the mud and sand at the water's edge. A smaller number live where a river meets the sea.

Many freshwater bivalves live in mud.

The land

Shelled mollusks that live on the land are often called "land snails." There are approximately 24,000 species of land snails in the world. Land snails can be found in tropical forests, on farmland, up mountains, in deserts, and even deep inside caves.

A land snail breaks down limestone rock and converts it into a shell.

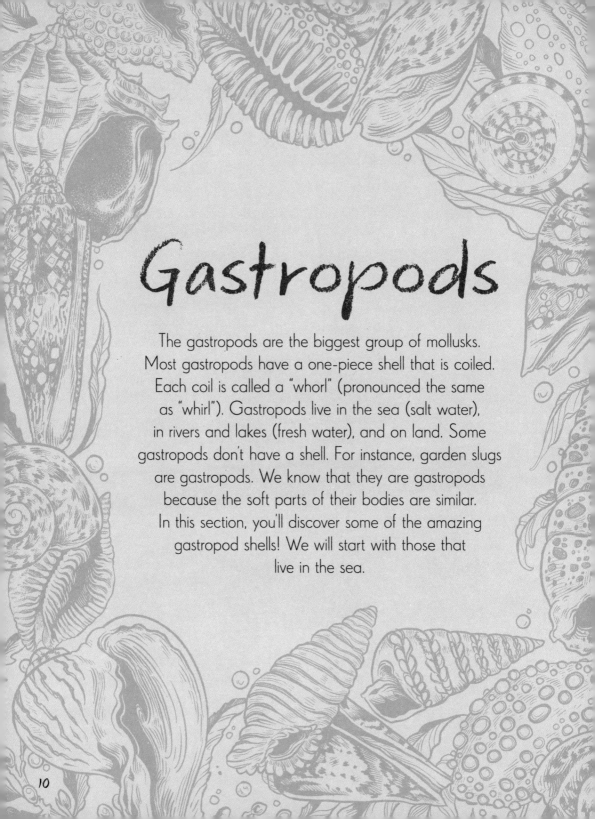

Gastropods

The gastropods are the biggest group of mollusks. Most gastropods have a one-piece shell that is coiled. Each coil is called a "whorl" (pronounced the same as "whirl"). Gastropods live in the sea (salt water), in rivers and lakes (fresh water), and on land. Some gastropods don't have a shell. For instance, garden slugs are gastropods. We know that they are gastropods because the soft parts of their bodies are similar. In this section, you'll discover some of the amazing gastropod shells! We will start with those that live in the sea.

Habitat: Marine

Ringed top

Calliostoma annulatum

The top shells usually have bright colors, like this ringed top shell. The animals inside them move around on the seabed, eating seaweed and corals. They carry their shell with them and are never able to leave it entirely. When threatened, the animal will shelter inside its shell.

Apex (the top of the shell)

Operculum (closes the aperture, almost like a trapdoor)

Aperture (the opening where the animal can emerge)

Notes

- Top shells are the same shape as a spinning top, which is how they got their name.

- If you hold the shell with its apex pointing up, the aperture will be on the right. Most gastropods coil in this direction.

Habitat: Marine

Spotted top
Clanculus stigmatarius

Many of the top shells have a surface that is covered in beads or "pustules." These often have different colors. The spotted top is easy to recognize because two spirals on each whorl include red beads.

Beaded sculpture

Notes
- The inner surface of top shells is shiny and changes color with the angle of the light. This is called "iridescence."
- Like many top shells, the spotted top lives in shallow water on rocks.

Toothlike projections protect the animal inside.

Iridescent inner surface

12

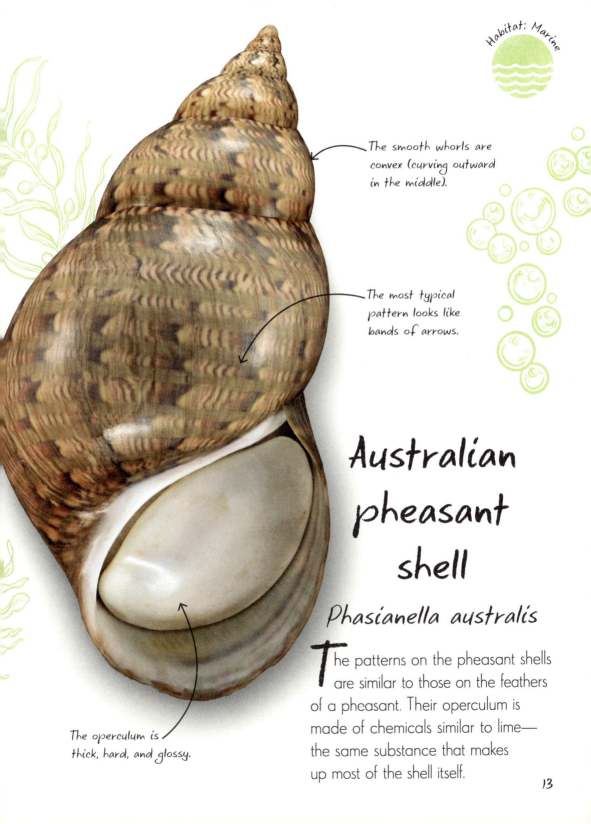

Habitat: Marine

The smooth whorls are convex (curving outward in the middle).

The most typical pattern looks like bands of arrows.

The operculum is thick, hard, and glossy.

Australian pheasant shell

Phasianella australis

The patterns on the pheasant shells are similar to those on the feathers of a pheasant. Their operculum is made of chemicals similar to lime—the same substance that makes up most of the shell itself.

Habitat: Marine

Hollow spines fan out at the ends.

The typical size of the shell is 2.5 in (60 mm).

Girdled star shell

Bolma girgyllus

The star shells are related to the top shells. When you look down on them, they have a star shape. The hard spines that grow outward from the girdled star shell are sometimes called "fronds," because they fan out at the ends like the leaves of some plants. The operculum is thick and white, like that of a pheasant shell.

Habitat: Marine

Long-spined dolphin shell

Angaria vicdani

The dolphin shells look similar to the star shells, but their operculum is thin and dark brown. The long-spined dolphin shell has a low spire (the shell's earlier whorls) but has spectacular spines that usually turn upward. The spines are very fragile, and no single shell is perfect!

Low spire

Thin, circular operculum

Notes

- The color is usually a mixture of green and red.
- When this shell's animal is alive, the spines are covered in smaller sea creatures.

Habitat: Marine

Orange color inside

Columella

Bleeding tooth

Nerita peloronta

It is easy to see how this shell gets its name! Three grooves in the columella (the central pillar of a gastropod) make it look like the shell has human teeth, and there is always a red stain there. These shells and their relatives are called nerites, and they can be very common on rocky shores.

Notes

• The operculum has a "hinge" on the back, so the animal can emerge from its shell while its operculum stays in place.

• Like many nerites, the bleeding tooth can live happily on dry rocks when the tide is out.

Moriori abalone

Haliotis virginea morioria

The abalones (or ormers) are quite flat, yet you can still see that they are coiled shells. These mollusks fix themselves to rocks but can crawl around. This shell comes from the island of Rēkohu, near New Zealand, and so it is named after the first people to settle there—the Moriori.

Habitat: Marine

The inside of the shell is coated with rainbow-colored mother-of-pearl, or "nacre."

The color may vary with what the animal has eaten.

A row of holes allows the animal to extract oxygen from seawater.

17

South African keyhole limpet

Diodora elizabethae

Habitat: Marine

Instead of a row of holes, the animal "breathes" through a single keyhole.

Unlike most gastropod shells, the limpets and keyhole limpets are not coiled. Instead, their shells are cone-shaped, and the animal clamps down onto rocks. This keeps them safe from predators, and it allows them to survive in rough waves.

The typical size of the shell is 1.5 in (40 mm).

Strong "ribs" (ridges on the shell's surface)

Habitat: Marine

Notes

- The typical length of the shell is 3.5 in (90 mm).
- This shell is found in eastern Australia and the Philippines, usually living among seagrass.

Prince's horn shell

Pseudovertagus phylarchus

Most of the horn shells live in shallow water around the seashore, sometimes in large colonies. Their shells are elongated, and they have a deep channel at the base called the "siphonal canal," where water travels in and out. Many horn shells are dull in color, but the prince's horn shell has an eye-catching pattern.

Waste canal

Columella extends partly across the patterned part of the shell

Siphonal canal

19

Habitat: Brackish

The shell's apex normally drops off.

West African mud creeper

Tympanotonus fuscatus

Here is a mollusk that can live in brackish water, which is neither salty nor fresh. Where a large river reaches the sea, the saltiness of the water can change as the tide rises and falls. This is a challenging place for most animals to live, but the mud creepers thrive here.

Notes

- The color can be brown, black, or white, and some shells can have colored bands.

- Several West African countries have included this shell on their postage stamps.

Crinkled, or "crenulated," lip

Habitat: Marine

Early whorls are regular and separated from one another.

Hefty screw shell

Tenagodus ponderosus

When it's young, this screw shell looks like most gastropods. As it gets older, it suddenly starts to grow in a bizarre way, without normal coils. So each individual shell will be a different shape. Some of these animals live in large colonies with their shells tangling up together.

Here, the normal coiling stops.

A slit runs the whole length of the shell.

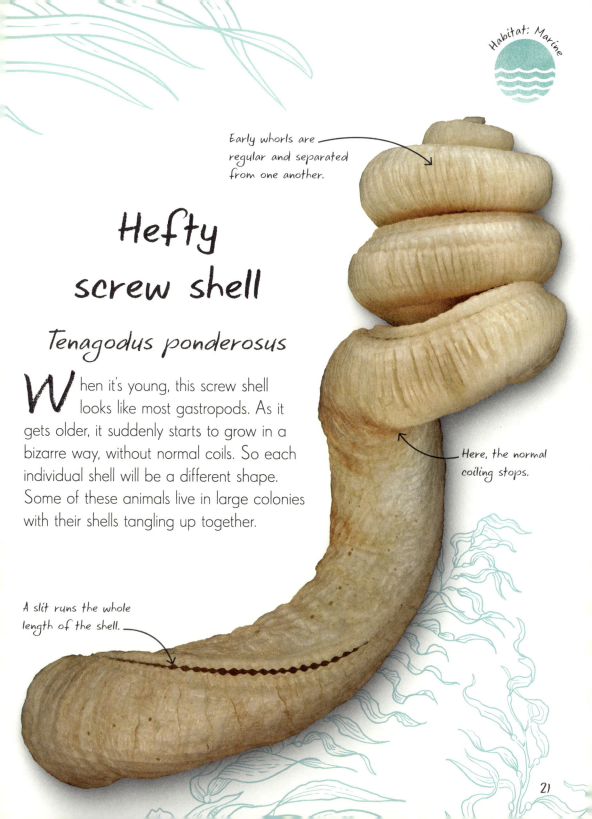

21

Habitat: Marine

Vomer conch

Euprotomus vomer

The true conchs are mostly quite large, heavy mollusks that live on sand and can bury themselves in it. All of them have a smooth notch near the siphonal canal, called the "stromboid notch."

Ribbed aperture

One of the animal's eyes pokes out from the stromboid notch and one from the siphonal canal.

Stromboid notch

Bull conch

Latissistrombus taurus

The bull conch gets its name from the two "spines" that project from its upper lip. These resemble the horns of a bull. Like a bull, the bull conch is very solid and heavy, yet the animal can move around surprisingly fast.

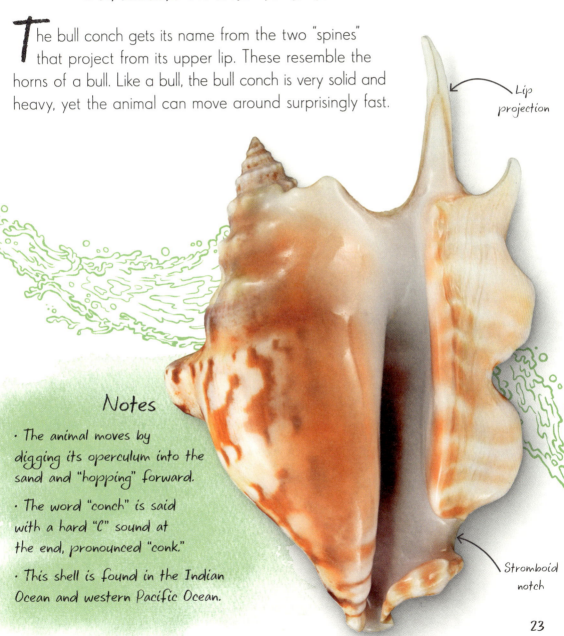

Lip projection

Stromboid notch

Notes

- The animal moves by digging its operculum into the sand and "hopping" forward.
- The word "conch" is said with a hard "C" sound at the end, pronounced "conk."
- This shell is found in the Indian Ocean and western Pacific Ocean.

Habitat: Marine

Habitat: Marine

The lip projection almost merges with the shell's spire.

Long siphonal canal

Stromboid notch

Fingered spider conch
Ophioglossolambis digitata

The spider conchs might not appear very similar to the true conchs, but they are close relatives. They have a stromboid notch, just like the true conchs. The lip projections sometimes look a bit like the legs of a spider, and in this shell, they look like fingers.

Miraculous soft-cap

Torellia mirabilis

The warm, tropical seas contain the biggest variety of seashells. However, seashells can also live in the very coldest waters on Earth. This soft-cap shell is truly miraculous, found at the bottom of the Weddell Sea and the Ross Sea, which surround Antarctica.

Habitat: Marine

Velvety "skin" consisting of fine hairs, called the "periostracum"

Large aperture

"Reflected" lip (the lip curves outward)

Notes

· The shell itself is so soft that when you pick it up it feels squishy.

· It is so difficult for scientists to explore the seas around Antarctica that many amazing animals have rarely been seen by any human.

25

Shell collectors of the sea

Throughout history, people have collected shells for all sorts of reasons. But there are actually shells that collect shells! These mollusks are called the "carrier shells," because they carry around pieces of other shells and rocks on their own shell.

Rough carrier shell

This rough carrier shell (*Xenophora corrugata*) chooses to collect pieces of bivalve shells. The shell itself is almost completely covered, apart from underneath. The animal deliberately attaches each piece that it selects for its "collection."

Pieces of bivalve shells

Each piece takes about 10 hours to attach.

Pale carrier shell

The pale carrier shell (*Xenophora pallidula*) collects whatever is available! It picks up various other shells and also some pieces of mineral. The attachments probably help the animal to blend in with its surroundings.

West African carrier shell

The West African carrier shell (*Xenophora senegalensis*) collects small stones, never shells. The shell's most recent addition lifts the animal off the seabed, allowing it to feed easily without exposing it to predators. This is probably the most important reason carrier shells acquire attachments.

Small stones, not shells, are collected.

Chinese carrier shell

The Chinese carrier shell (*Xenophora chinensis*) collects only small shells. Mostly it collects delicate bivalves. Around the apex, the bivalve attachments are tiny, and the carrier shell chooses bigger ones as it grows.

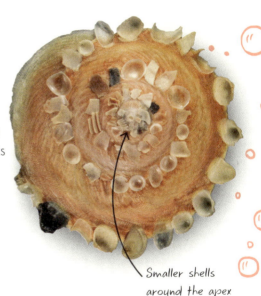

Smaller shells around the apex

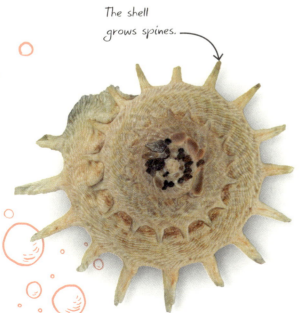

The shell grows spines.

Spiny carrier shell

The spiny carrier shell (*Stellaria paucispinosa*) picks up attachments only when it is young. As it gets older, it grows spines, which might have the same purpose as the attachments. So with this type, we can actually see the surface of the carrier shell itself.

Habitat: Marine

"Teeth" may protect the animal inside

Narrow aperture

The smooth, rounded back has a zigzag pattern but, unlike the base, has no spots.

Zigzag cowrie

Palmadusta ziczac

People have admired the cowrie shells for thousands of years. Perhaps it is because they are always shiny! They feel as if they have been "polished." Often, cowries are named after the pattern on their back, such as with this zigzag cowrie.

Habitat: Marine

Golden cowrie

Callistocypraea aurantium

The golden cowrie is very easy to recognize because of its bright-orange back. In the past, it was a difficult shell to find, and the owner of one would be greatly admired. It is also called the "morning dawn cowrie."

Notes

- The side of a gastropod shell that has the aperture is called the "ventrum," but with cowries, it's also called the "base."

- The golden cowrie's beautiful color tends to fade over several years.

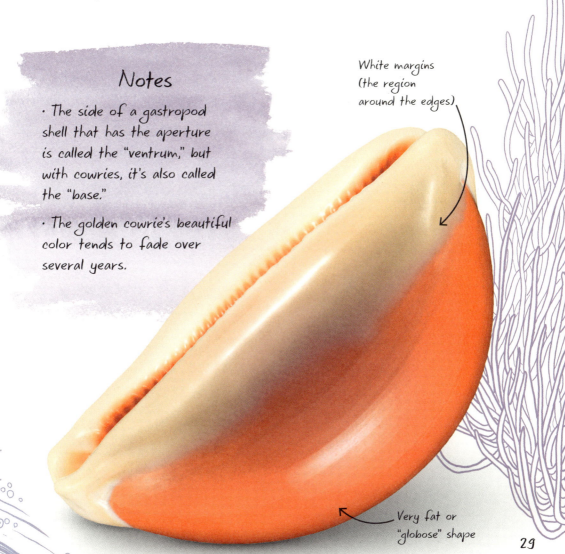

White margins (the region around the edges)

Very fat or "globose" shape

29

Habitat: Marine

Great spotted cowrie

Perisserosa guttata

Many cowries have spots on their backs. The combination of white spots on an orange back makes this shell especially eye-catching. Like all the cowries, the shell is covered when it moves around by a soft part of the animal called the "mantle."

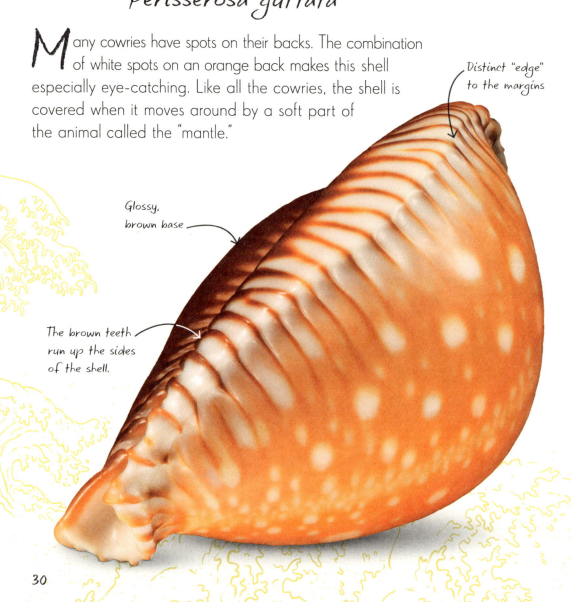

Distinct "edge" to the margins

Glossy, brown base

The brown teeth run up the sides of the shell.

The pattern on the back looks like a Maltese cross.

Habitat: Marine

The grainy surface is very unusual for a cowrie.

Maltese cross cowrie

Barycypraea fultoni

This mysterious cowrie is taken from the stomachs of large fish! The black musselcracker fish eats these shells, and the acids in its stomach kill the living mollusk. The shell itself may survive, and could then be discovered by a fisherman.

The pattern of four arrowheads pointing inward is called a "Maltese cross."

Habitat: Marine

Notes

- This cowrie is named after the Cape of Good Hope, near the very southern tip of the African continent.
- South Africa is where the Atlantic Ocean meets the Indian Ocean, and this creates habitats for many different shells.

No teeth on the columella

Cape cowrie

Cypraeovula capensis

Several types of cowries around South Africa have teeth on only one side of the aperture. And there is something else unusual about the Cape cowrie—it has ridges all around it instead of being completely smooth. The color can be anything from pale tan to dark purple.

Spiral ridges wrap all around

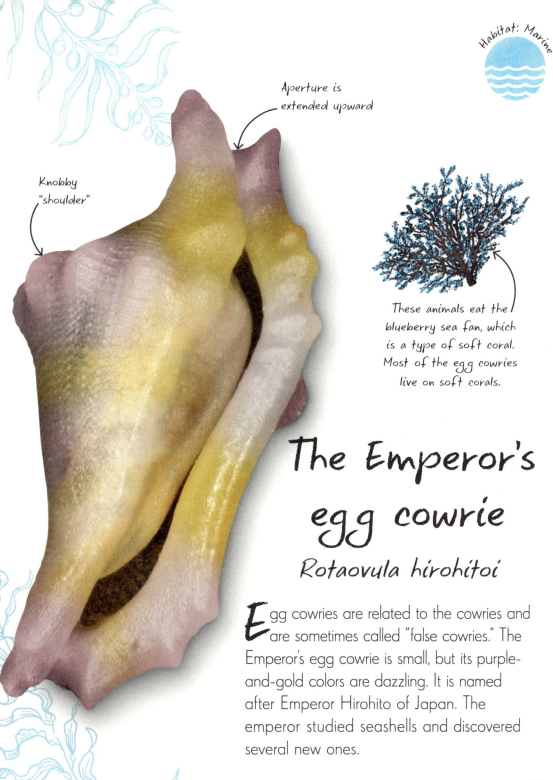

Habitat: Marine

Aperture is extended upward

Knobby "shoulder"

These animals eat the blueberry sea fan, which is a type of soft coral. Most of the egg cowries live on soft corals.

The Emperor's egg cowrie
Rotaovula hirohitoi

Egg cowries are related to the cowries and are sometimes called "false cowries." The Emperor's egg cowrie is small, but its purple-and-gold colors are dazzling. It is named after Emperor Hirohito of Japan. The emperor studied seashells and discovered several new ones.

Habitat: Marine

Each pustule is surrounded by a dark ring.

White ribs extend right across the base.

Blistered egg cowrie
Jenneria pustulata

This startling shell is another relative of the cowries. The base has strong, white ribs. The back is covered in orange pustules, which look like blisters. The mantle of the living animal has exactly the same pattern of orange blobs.

Notes

• These animals eat coral and can even damage certain coral reefs.

• Like many mollusks, the blistered egg cowrie is nocturnal (active only at night).

34

Violet moon shell

Tectonatica violacea

Habitat: Marine

Most moon shells are round or "globular," and the animal often appears too big for its shell. These mollusks live in the sand and can burrow. They are predatory animals—they hunt other mollusks, mostly bivalves. They produce an acid that bores a hole in their chosen target and suck out their prey from inside!

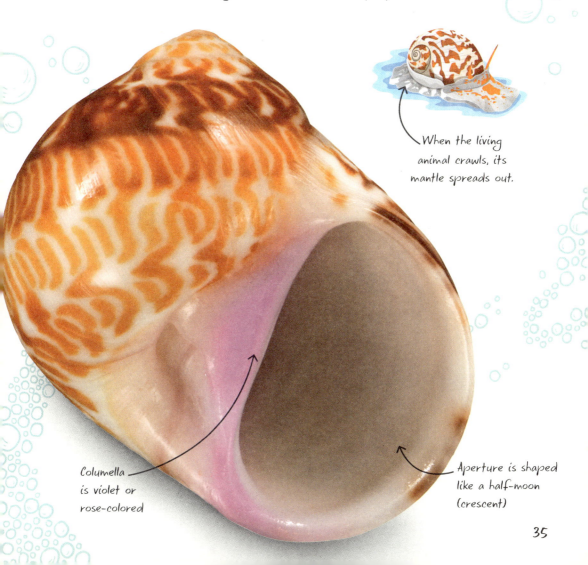

When the living animal crawls, its mantle spreads out.

Columella is violet or rose-colored

Aperture is shaped like a half-moon (crescent)

35

Habitat: Marine

Pot-bellied fig

Ficus ventricosus

The pot-bellied fig shell looks swollen and might remind you of the fruit of the same name. It spends most of its time buried in the sand. The animal inside has a large mantle, which is the organ actually responsible for making the shell. If part of the mantle is destroyed by a predator, it will grow back!

Low spire

Spiraling ribs are known as "cords."

When the animal is crawling on the sand, you can see the mantle, which is gray with white spots.

Habitat: Marine

Toothlike ornaments, called "denticles," around the aperture

The aperture is wider at the bottom.

Galápagos helmet shell

Cypraecassis tenuis

Most helmet shells are quite large and heavy. The Galápagos helmet shell has a low spire, but the "body whorl" (the shell's final coil at its base) is huge. The Galápagos Islands are a group of small islands in the eastern Pacific Ocean. They are home to an amazing variety of wildlife.

Notes

- The typical height of the shell is 4.5 in (11 cm).
- Female Galápagos helmet shells are much bigger than males.
- Some helmet shells can be used as musical instruments.

Musical shells

Some shells can be used to make music! People convert the largest gastropods into "horns," usually by breaking off the shell's apex and then blowing into the hole that's left. Other shells are sometimes converted into percussion instruments.

Pacific triton

The Pacific triton (*Charonia tritonis*) is a huge shell that makes an impressive, booming sound. A skilled musician can produce different notes by tightening their lips. This is exactly the same technique that a trumpet player would use, but it takes some practice!

This is one of the largest gastropod shells.

Peruvian conch

The Peruvian conch (*Titanostrombus galeatus*) was used as a horn by the Chavín people for special occasions. The Chavín people lived in Peru more than 2,200 years ago. Other conchs like the queen conch are still used as horns today in the Caribbean.

Ancient people carved drawings into the shell.

Knobbed triton

This actual shell was used as a musical instrument by people 17,000 years ago! They lived in a cave in what is now modern-day France. It is a knobbed triton (*Charonia lampas*), from the Mediterranean Sea. It is one of the oldest musical instruments ever found, and it is now in a museum in Toulouse, France.

Ancient musicians probably fixed a "mouthpiece" into the apex.

The Indian chank is one of several large shells used to make music in India.

Indian chank

The Indian chank (*Turbinella pyrum*) is an important symbol in the Hindu and Buddhist religions. Religious artwork often shows gods and goddesses blowing chanks. In India, it is known as a *shankha*, and if made into a trumpet, it might have a mouthpiece. The *shankha* is blown to mark special events.

Ringed cowries (*Monetaria annulus*) are often used for these instruments.

Cowries as percussion

You can make a percussion instrument by fastening small cowries around the outside of a dried gourd fruit. When you shake it, it makes a pleasing rhythmic sound. In West Africa, this instrument is called a *shekere*. It is popular in other parts of the world, too.

Habitat: Marine

The hairs are part of the periostracum.

The periostracum between the hairs looks like transparent wings.

Winged triton
Cabestana felipponei

Many shells have a thin layer of "skin" on their outside, called the periostracum. Usually it is lost quickly after the animal dies. In the triton shells, this periostracum is thick and usually hairy. Shells such as the winged triton have a special texture when held in the hands.

Neapolitan triton

Monoplex parthenopeus

The Neapolitan triton has a thick, rugged periostracum over its solid, heavy shell. Very unusually, it can be found in almost all the world's warm seas. It is easy to recognize from the black-and-white markings in its aperture.

Habitat: Marine

Notes

- The very young animal, the "veliger," can swim freely for many weeks before its shell starts growing and it settles down.
- The veliger's ability to swim explains how this shell has spread over such a wide area.

Denticles on the lip

Very thick periostracum with hairs

Habitat: Marine

Robinson's distortion shell

Distorsio robinsoni

The distortion shells are closely related to the tritons. They always appear to have a twisted aperture, and the front of the shell is flat. This gives the shell an odd, squished appearance. All distortion shells have a thick layer of periostracum.

Notes

- Robinson's distortion shell has long hairs, which are actually part of the periostracum.
- The substances that make up the periostracum are similar to those in the cuticle of your fingernails.

Fuzzy periostracum

The large denticles make the aperture narrow.

The glossy area around the columella is called the "parietal shield."

Lamarck's frog shell
Bursa lamarckii

Habitat: Marine

The frog shells have heavy knobs called "tubercles," which remind some people of warty skin, like a frog's. This shell is solid and robust. The animal creates a new lip after each half-turn that it grows, and this gives the shell a special symmetrical shape.

Tubercle

Waste canal

Some frogs have bumps on their skin that look like warts or blisters.

Denticles on the lip

43

Habitat: Marine

Splendid niso

Niso splendidula

The niso shells are part of a very large group of mollusks that are parasitic. This means they live on the body of another animal and cause harm to that animal. The niso shells live on the outside of sea stars and suck out their body fluid.

- Zigzag pattern
- Very glossy surface
- Teardrop-shaped operculum

Sea stars, such as this red cushion star, are targets for the parasitic niso shells.

44

Habitat: Marine

Common wentletrap

Epitonium clathrus

The wentletraps are delicate and very elegant. Most of them have several ribs on each whorl—these ribs are the previous lips that the animal has made as it has grown. Most wentletraps are white, but the common wentletrap is often brown or has brown bands.

— There is a small gap between the whorls.

— Rib

Notes

• The English word "wentletrap" comes from a Dutch word that means "spiral staircase."

• Wentletraps are parasitic, like the niso shells, and they attack sea anemones.

45

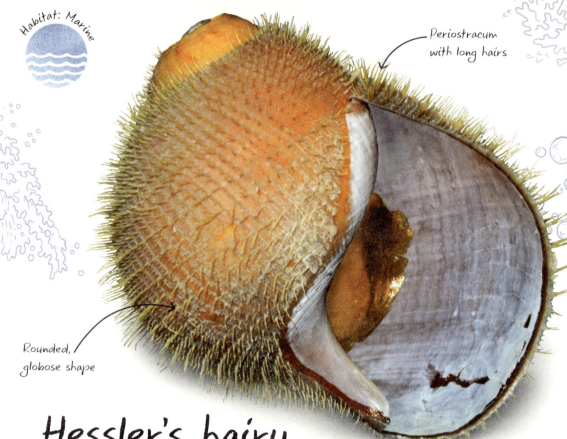

Habitat: Marine

Periostracum with long hairs

Rounded, globose shape

Hessler's hairy vent shell

Alviniconcha hessleri

Mollusks can live in the very deepest parts of the ocean. No light ever reaches there, and very few animals can survive. We are only just beginning to explore these places, with special submarines and robotic devices. This hairy vent shell came from 2.2 miles (3.6 km) deep in an ocean trench.

Notes

- The hairs grow in a perfect grid pattern.
- These animals live around cracks, or "vents," in the ocean floor, where boiling water blows out of the Earth's crust!

Habitat: Marine

Checkerboard goblet shell

Engina alveolata

The goblet shells are related to the whelks. This one gets its name from the arrangement of black bumps, or "nodes," that look like the pattern of a checkerboard. It is quite common in warm, shallow water.

Double row of orange nodes

Double row of black nodes

Looking from above, you see a beautiful pattern of orange-and-black nodes.

Dark-red lip and columella, with white denticles

Habitat: Marine

Japanese corded whelk

Ancistrolepis grammata

The English word "whelk" can be confusing because it is used for several different groups of shells. This is one of the "true whelks." Most whelks are not colorful, but they can have a beautiful sculpture—like the Japanese corded whelk.

The operculum is almost triangular.

Cord

Channel

48

Habitat: Marine

Notes
- Torr's whelk is probably not a "true whelk," but it is a close relative.
- Most shells from southern Australia can't be found in other parts of the world. However, most shells from northern Australia can also be found in the Indian and the Pacific Ocean.

Torr's whelk
Godfreyena luculenta

This whelk from warm waters in southern Australia is very easy to recognize. It has a wide band that is orange or peach in color. There are brown dots and squiggly brown markings, which are sometimes called "flames." When you pick up the shell, you can feel that it has very delicate spiral cords.

Brown "flame" markings

Brown dots

Siphonal canal twists sharply

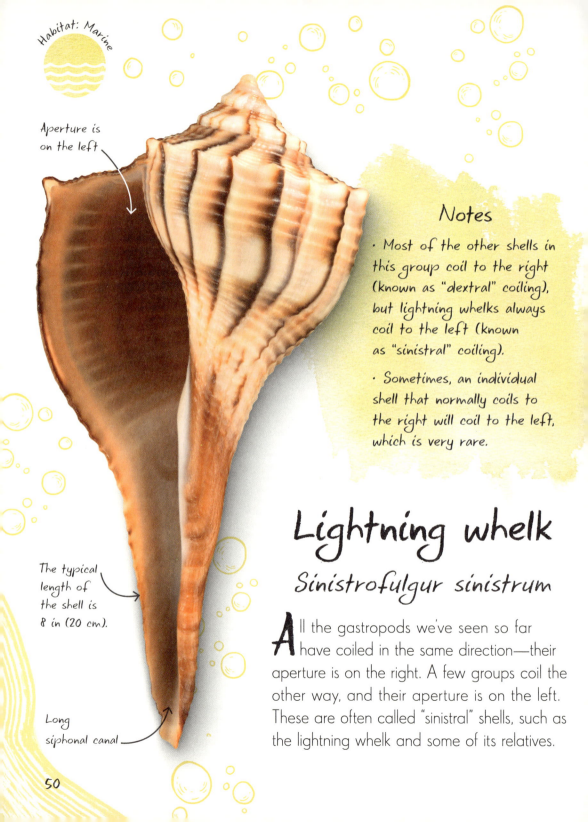

Habitat: Marine

Aperture is on the left

The typical length of the shell is 8 in (20 cm).

Long siphonal canal

Notes

• Most of the other shells in this group coil to the right (known as "dextral" coiling), but lightning whelks always coil to the left (known as "sinistral" coiling).

• Sometimes, an individual shell that normally coils to the right will coil to the left, which is very rare.

Lightning whelk

Sinistrofulgur sinistrum

All the gastropods we've seen so far have coiled in the same direction—their aperture is on the right. A few groups coil the other way, and their aperture is on the left. These are often called "sinistral" shells, such as the lightning whelk and some of its relatives.

Habitat: Marine

Lined spindle shell
Serratifusus lineatus

The lined spindle belongs to a small group of similar mollusks that live in deep water. They can be found in a part of the Pacific Ocean (near New Caledonia), where fishing boats don't go, and very few sailors visit. Therefore, we don't often see the beautiful shells that live in these waters.

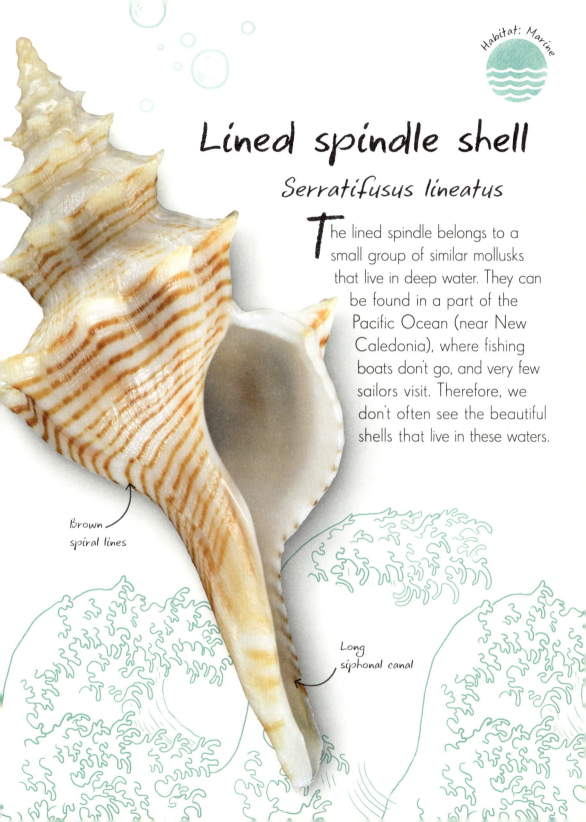

Brown spiral lines

Long siphonal canal

Habitat: Marine

Splendid dove shell

Pyrene splendidula

The dove shells are a large group of rather small shells. They can be really common along the shoreline, and so they are shells that lots of people see. Many of them have small denticles on the inside of the lip, like this splendid dove shell.

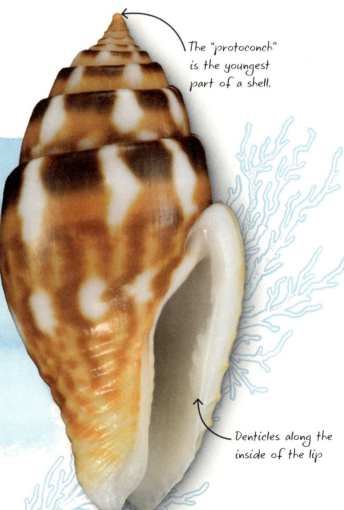

The "protoconch" is the youngest part of a shell.

Notes

• The "protoconch" often has a very different structure from the rest of the shell.

• Some types of shells lose their protoconchs as they grow, but the dove shells don't.

Denticles along the inside of the lip

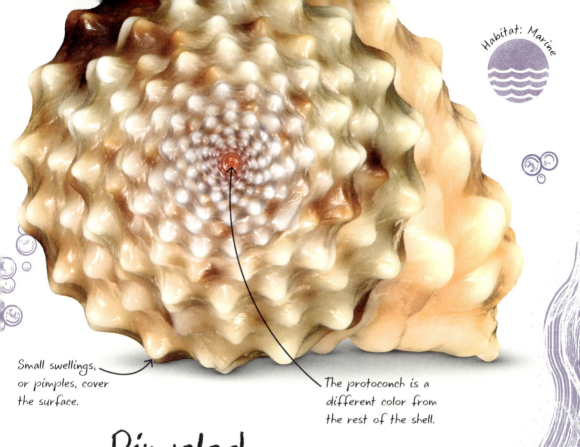

Habitat: Marine

Small swellings, or pimples, cover the surface.

The protoconch is a different color from the rest of the shell.

Pimpled mud shell

Nassarius papillosus

Mollusks in this group thrive in muddy and sandy places, usually close to the shore. Sometimes they live in huge colonies. Many of the shells have ribs on their whorls, but the pimpled mud shell is covered in a regular arrangement of small swellings.

The animal glides gracefully over the mud as it searches for food.

Habitat: Marine

Glossy purple columella, which extends across the shell

Fine spiral lines in the aperture

Tubercles on the shell's shoulder

Persian horse conch

Pleuroploca clava

The horse conchs are not related to the true conchs. They are large and heavy shells with broad siphonal canals. The Persian horse conch has a particularly colorful shell. These animals eat other mollusks!

Festive mini-spindle

Teralatirus roboreus

The festive mini-spindle belongs to a very small group of similar shells. Experts used to believe they were in a different group, the vase shells. However, they are probably more closely related to the true whelks. This shell is small, but the combination of different-colored bands is startling.

Habitat: Marine

Notes

- The festive mini-spindle lives underneath blocks of broken coral in shallow water.

- You would be most likely to see this shell in the Lesser Antilles islands, or around the small islands off Venezuela.

Two red-brown folds on the columella

Red-brown marks on the lip

Protected shells

Some shells are protected by laws—we cannot normally collect them. There is an agreement between countries of the world that protects particular shells. Here are some that are protected all around the world.

Queen conch

Queen conchs (*Aliger gigas*) have been overcollected because people like to eat the animals. This means there are fewer queen conchs around. Now, they are protected.

These shells can be used to make music!

Strawberry clam

Giant clams, such as this strawberry clam (*Hippopus hippopus*), are all protected by international law. The giant clams can be very common in tropical reefs, where they embed themselves in between corals. Anyone forcing a shell out of the reef would damage the corals.

O'ahu tree snails

Many colorful tree snails used to live in the mountains of O'ahu, Hawaii. Sadly, predators that ate the snails were accidentally brought to the island, so some of the snails are now extinct. All those that remain are protected.

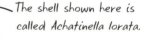

The shell shown here is called *Achatinella lorata*.

Pearly nautilus

Fishermen used to collect large quantities of pearly nautilus (*Nautilus pompilius*) and sell them to tourists as souvenirs. Despite having a coiled shell, these mollusks are not gastropods, but cephalopods.

One-piece shell that is coiled, like a gastropod

This snail is called the charming Polymita (*Polymita venusta*).

Polymita snails

In the past, Polymita snails were collected to make jewelry. The land they live on is also being changed by farmers. All of the Polymita snails, found only on the Caribbean island of Cuba, are now protected species.

Emerald green tree snail

The emerald green tree snail (*Papustyla pulcherrima*) lives only on one small island near Papua New Guinea. It lives high in the trees, and unfortunately many of the trees have been cut down.

These shells have also been taken to make jewelry.

Freshwater shells

Several freshwater bivalves, such as the western fanshell (*Cyprogenia aberti*), are also protected.

The list of all protected shells sometimes changes, and some shells are protected in only some countries, but not others!

Habitat: Marine

This murex has spines that look like the sprouting leaves of a rose bush.

Main spines end in pink fronds

There are spines on the siphonal canal.

Rose-branch murex

Chicoreus palmarosae

The murex shells are one of the biggest and most important groups of gastropods. They are also a very varied group. Many of them have elaborate spines. The most beautiful examples of the rose-branch murex come from Sri Lanka.

Orchid murex

Chicoreus orchidiflorus

Habitat: Marine

Rather than spines, the orchid murex has a greatly expanded lip that looks like a fin or a wing. The shell forms a lip three times for each whorl that it grows. The previous lips are easy to see and they are called "varices" (one on its own is called a "varix").

An old lip, or varix.

Extended current lip

Notes

- Two of the shell's previous siphonal canals can also be seen. One of them curves left, and the other curves toward you.

- Like most murex shells, the orchid murex feeds on other mollusks.

Curved siphonal canal

Habitat: Marine

Columella extends upward

Notes

- The spines prevent this shell from sinking into the mud where it's found.
- The spines also discourage predators of this mollusk.

Venus comb

Murex pecten

The long spines of this murex look very much like a comb for your hair. Venus was the Roman goddess of love. So supposedly, this shell is the comb that a goddess would use! The shell is actually quite difficult to pick up without hurting yourself.

Very long siphonal canal

Habitat: Marine

Varix

Ruffled lip extension

Denticles on the lip and on the columella

Club murex

Pterynotus elongatus

The club murex has a beautifully ruffled extension to its lip. The shell's previous lips form varices that seem to be arranged in a regular line up the shell. Often the varices are worn down during the animal's lifetime, so no shell looks perfect.

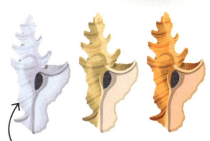

The club murex can be of different colors—white (the most common), yellow, orange, and violet.

Habitat: Marine

Butterfly murex

Timbellus bednalli

This exquisite murex has very well-developed varices. Usually the varices are lined up down the spire of the shell, giving the appearance of perfect "wings." These "wings" are so large that it looks as if the aperture is too small for the shell.

Notes

• Aboriginal Australians call this the "butterfly shell" because its varices look like the wings of a butterfly.

• The color can be pink, white, orange, or brown, and sometimes a mix of these colors.

Varices almost completely cover the shell's apex

Double row of denticles on the lip

Habitat: Marine

Tubelike waste canal

Round aperture with a raised rim

Tubelike siphonal canal

For a ballet dancer, this is called the "Arabesque penchée" position.

Pavlova's typhis

Siphonochelus pavlova

Typhis shells have a long tube for expelling waste. In Pavlova's typhis, this tube appears to stick almost straight up, like a ballet dancer with one leg raised above their head! It is named after Anna Pavlova, a famous Russian ballerina.

Habitat: Marine

Burnett's thorn-mouth
Ceratostoma burnettii

This murex and its relatives are sometimes called the "thorn-mouths," because they have a projection on the lip that looks like a thorn. Like all the murex shells, they are predators. They use their thorn to open up bivalve shells so that they can eat the animal inside.

Varix

"Thorn"

Notes
- The color can be brown, tan, orange, or white, and some shells have spiral bands.
- This shell is found in Korea, northern China, and Japan.

Habitat: Marine

The typical size of the shell is 1 in (25 mm).

The longest spine is on the lip.

The aperture is almost triangular.

The points and tiers on a Japanese pagoda resemble the spines of this shell.

Spiny coral shell

Babelomurex jeanneae

The coral shells are closely related to murex shells, but these mollusks eat corals. The spiny coral shell has a regular arrangement of up-turned spines. Some people believe that these spines inspired ancient Japanese designers, because some Japanese pagodas look quite similar.

Habitat: Marine

Each whorl has a sharp ridge called a keel, or a "carina."

Apricot-colored aperture

You can see the massive size of this shell when it's held in someone's hands.

False trumpet shell

Syrinx aruana

This is the largest gastropod shell, sometimes reaching 27.5 in (70 cm) long! It is so big that Australians often use false trumpet shells as plant pots, or just to decorate their gardens. The false trumpet is not related to the trumpet shells. It belongs to a group called the vase shells.

Habitat: Marine

Zanzibar vase

Tudivasum zanzibaricum

This beautiful vase shell has a very thick lip and a large parietal shield. Young shells just have a thin lip and no parietal shield. Many of the vase shells have knobs on the shoulder, but this is one of the few that is truly spiny.

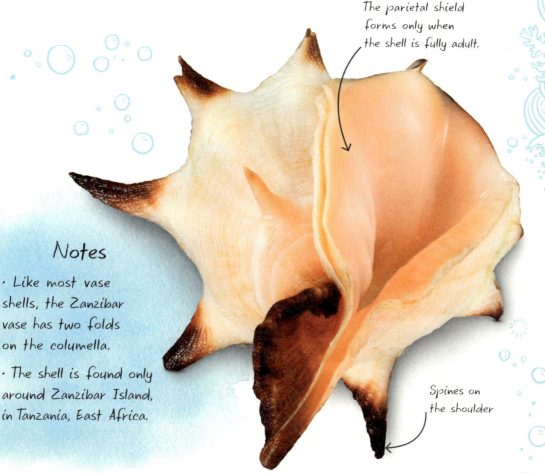

The parietal shield forms only when the shell is fully adult.

Notes
- Like most vase shells, the Zanzibar vase has two folds on the columella.
- The shell is found only around Zanzibar Island, in Tanzania, East Africa.

Spines on the shoulder

Habitat: Marine

Protoconch is curled and elongated

Spiky pagoda shell

Columbarium hystriculum

The pagoda shells are all delicate shells with very long siphonal canals. Surprisingly, they are related to the much heavier vase shells. The spiky pagoda shell can be found only in very deep water, like all of the pagoda shells.

Very long siphonal canal with short spines

Notes

- Most of the pagoda shells are white or tan, but we can tell them apart from their sculpture of spines and keels.

- We see these mysterious mollusks only because sometimes they get caught up in fishing nets and are brought up to the surface.

Habitat: Marine

The typical size of the shell is only about 0.3 in (8 mm).

Axial ribs

Small ribs inside the aperture

Kuiper's ribbed miter

Vexillum kuiperi

The ribbed miters are a large group of colorful gastropods. Most of them have ribs that run up and down the whorls ("axial ribs"), rather than ribs that form spirals. Kuiper's ribbed miter has a startling pattern of red-and-white bands, separated by black spiral lines.

69

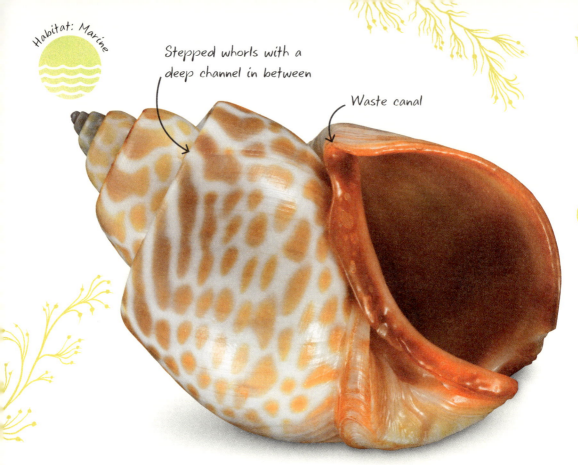

Habitat: Marine

Stepped whorls with a deep channel in between

Waste canal

Spiral Babylon

Babylonia spirata

The Babylons are a small group of shells that are always rather plump, or globose. Their whorls are rounded. The spiral Babylon has a pattern that is easy to recognize—reddish-brown blotches on a white background. It is a familiar shell on the Indian subcontinent because it washes up on beaches.

Notes

• Children sometimes turn this shell upside down and use it as a spinning top.

• There are about 20 different types of Babylon shells from around the world, yet the pattern is surprisingly similar among them all.

Onion shell
Melapium elatum

The very rounded shape of this shell reminds some people of an onion. The onion shells are a puzzling little group—experts cannot agree on which other shells they are similar to. They are all found in deep water off East and South Africa.

Habitat: Marine

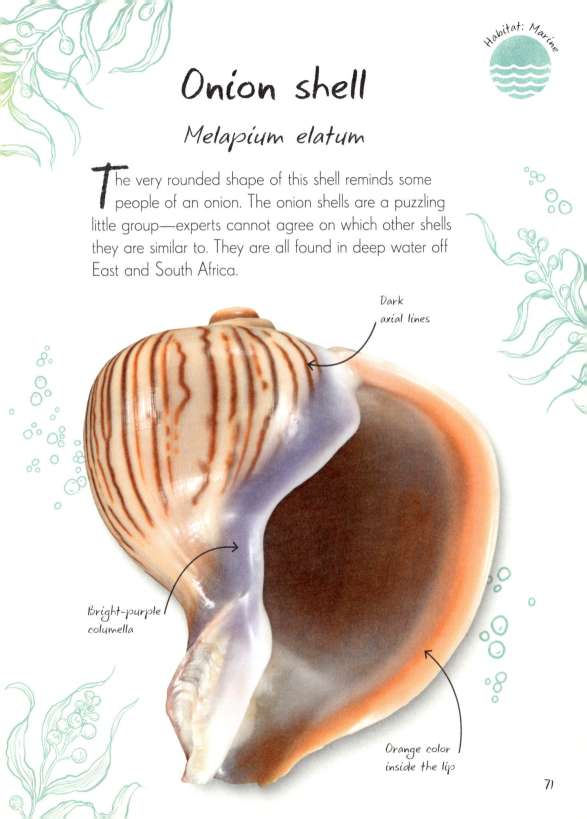

Dark axial lines

Bright-purple columella

Orange color inside the lip

Habitat: Marine

Three strong folds on the columella

Very thick, smooth lip

Festive volute

Festilyria casaana

The volutes are large and heavy shells. Their elegant shapes and patterns draw many admirers. The most colorful ones are found in warm waters, like this festive volute, but there are a few volutes that live in the Arctic and Antarctic regions.

Notes

• For many years, scientists were confused about where this volute lived. This was because shells were stored without labels showing where they were gathered.

• Like all the volutes, this animal is a predator—it eats small sea creatures.

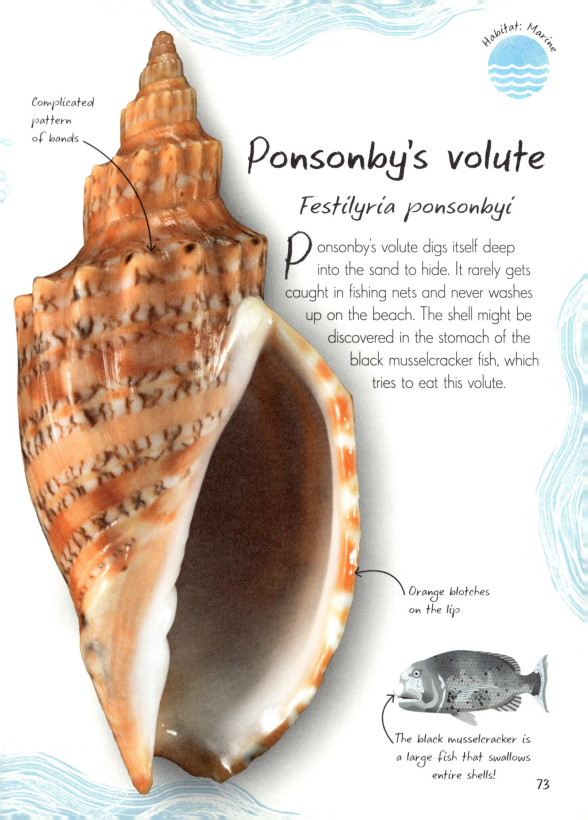

Habitat: Marine

Complicated pattern of bands

Ponsonby's volute
Festilyria ponsonbyi

Ponsonby's volute digs itself deep into the sand to hide. It rarely gets caught in fishing nets and never washes up on the beach. The shell might be discovered in the stomach of the black musselcracker fish, which tries to eat this volute.

Orange blotches on the lip

The black musselcracker is a large fish that swallows entire shells!

Habitat: Marine

Clover's volute

Lyria cloveriana

This beautifully colored volute lives only around Sri Lanka, in the Indian Ocean. The shells regularly get caught in fishermen's nets. Clover's volute is named after Phillip Clover, a famous shell expert in America who has discovered many new shells.

High spire with ribs and fine spiral lines

Notes

- Most volutes don't have an operculum, but this one does.
- The volutes are sometimes called "the millionaire shells" because some people are willing to pay large amounts of money for them.

Very small operculum

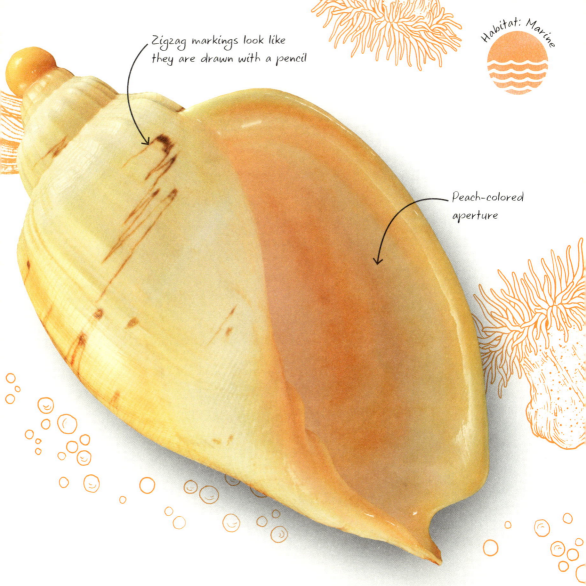

Mrs. Roadnight's volute
Livonia roadnightae

There was a lady named "Mrs. Roadnight," who found a volute on the beach and used it to prop open a window in her hotel. A scientist stayed in that same room, and he noticed this remarkable shell that he had never seen before! Eventually the shell was named in her honor—Mrs. Roadnight's volute.

Habitat: Marine

The typical size of the shell is 1.5 in (40 mm).

Prominent axial ribs

Love harp

Harpa amouretta

The harp shells are predatory animals with a large, muscular "foot" and an eye on each tentacle. Like all the harp shells, the love harp has broad axial ribs running from the top to the bottom of the body whorl. The aperture is large, but there is no operculum.

The animal uses its large "foot" to smother its prey.

Queen margin shell
Glabella pseudofaba

Habitat: Marine

The margin shells are a large group of striking shells, although many of them are quite small. They are very glossy. With their intricate patterns and varying colors, the margin shells can look like a collection of jewels. The queen margin shell always has a pattern of black spots.

Thick lip with many denticles

Very strong folds on the columella

Notes

- The most attractive margin shells come from western or southern Africa.
- The reason they are so glossy is that the animal's soft mantle covers the shell while it is moving.

Habitat: Marine

Uncoiled nutmeg

Trigonostoma milleri

The nutmeg shells are fairly small, usually brown, and they look a little bit like a nutmeg seed. The uncoiled nutmeg shell is very unusual because its whorls do not touch each other. This means that the central part of the shell is completely open, with the shell coiling around it.

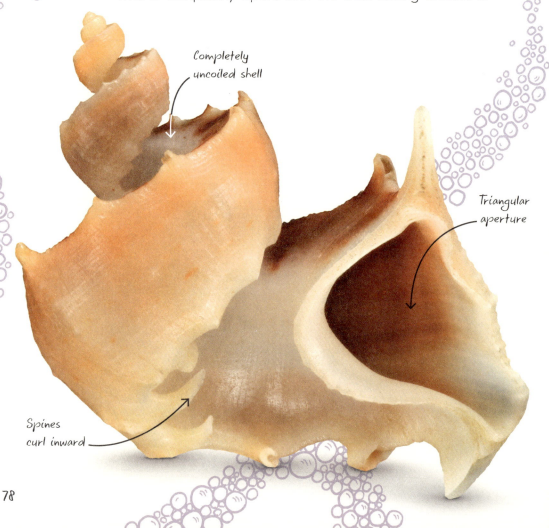

Completely uncoiled shell

Triangular aperture

Spines curl inward

Habitat: Marine

Notes

• True miters, such as this one, don't have axial ribs like the ribbed miters, although some of them do have spiral ribs.

• Like many mollusks, the miters are nocturnal animals. They are active only at night, looking for food to eat.

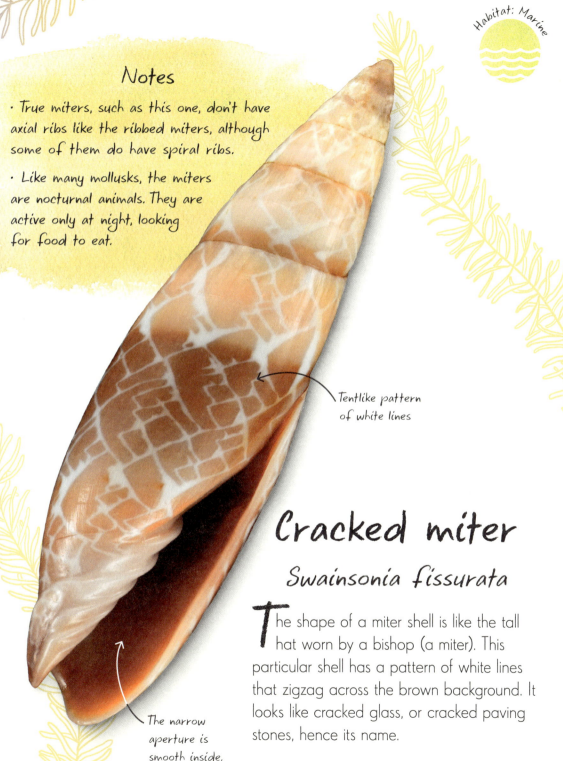

Tentlike pattern of white lines

The narrow aperture is smooth inside.

Cracked miter
Swainsonia fissurata

The shape of a miter shell is like the tall hat worn by a bishop (a miter). This particular shell has a pattern of white lines that zigzag across the brown background. It looks like cracked glass, or cracked paving stones, hence its name.

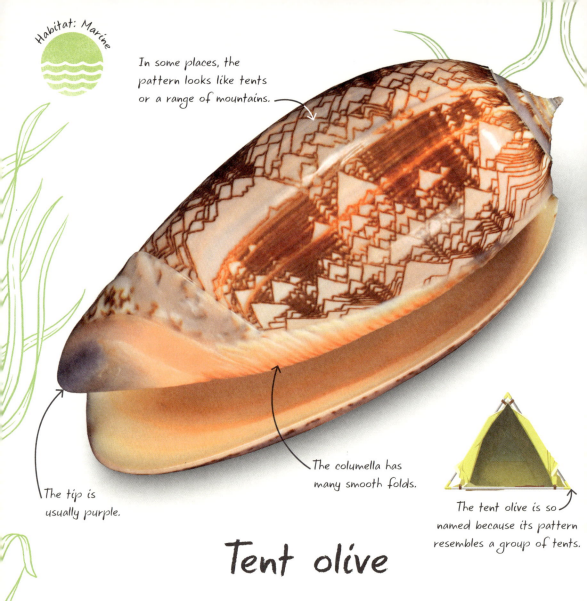

Habitat: Marine

In some places, the pattern looks like tents or a range of mountains.

The columella has many smooth folds.

The tip is usually purple.

The tent olive is so named because its pattern resembles a group of tents.

Tent olive

Oliva porphyria

This olive shell might remind you of a cowrie, but if you examine it closely, its aperture looks different. Olive shells come in many beautiful colors, but the tent olive is known for its pattern of sharp zigzags. This mollusk lives on sand and is active at night.

False olive

Amalda decipiens

The false olive has a thickened area of shell called a "callus." The callus reaches up onto the spire and covers the shell's earlier whorls, so that you cannot see the coiling. The lip is much thinner than the lip of an olive shell.

Habitat: Marine

Large callus

Notes

- The false olive and its relatives have an operculum, but the true olives never have an operculum.

- Like the true olives, the false olive attacks bivalve shells and sucks out the animal.

Purple columella

81

Habitat: Marine

Semicircular, white markings

Long, straight, and narrow aperture

Victor cone

Conus victor

People notice cone shells like this one because of their amazing patterns and attractive colors. The sides are often straight and they taper down to the siphonal canal, while the spire is often low. So the shape is like a cone. All the cones are predatory mollusks.

Textile cone
Conus textile

All cones are venomous to some extent, but the textile cone has killed people! The animal has a small "harpoon" and can inject venom very quickly. It is a very common shell, but it's one you definitely shouldn't pick up when the shell contains the animal.

Habitat: Marine

Brown areas, which form vague bands

Tented pattern

Notes

- The textile cone normally hunts for other mollusks, which it can consume whole.

- Out of about 1,000 types of cone shells in the world, this is one of five that are truly dangerous to humans.

The glory cones

The elegant shapes and intricate patterns of cone shells have long fascinated people. Over the years, certain cones have become some of the most desirable objects in nature. The shells on these pages have been given names that suit their high status.

The "Glory of the Seas" (*Conus gloriamaris*) was thought of as the most desirable seashell for centuries. It has a golden color and a very intricate tent pattern.

The "Glory of the Atlantic" (*Conus granulatus*) can be red, orange, or pink. It lives in the Caribbean Sea, in the western Atlantic. Notice its spiral sculpture (spiral cords).

This cone was discovered quite recently, in 2009, in the Philippines. With its golden color and fine pattern, it became known as the "Glory of the Ocean" (*Conus glorioceanus*).

The "Glory of Bengal" (*Conus bengalensis*) has a tent pattern like the Glory of India, but a lower spire. It is found in the Bay of Bengal.

One of the largest cones, the "Glory of India" (*Conus milneedwardsi*) can reach 7 in (18 cm) long. The spire is unusually high for a cone shell.

Habitat: Marine

Very fine, brown spiral lines

Purple siphonal canal

Notes

- The lip is thin, even though the shell is fully grown. Many other gastropods form a thick lip only when they are adults.
- Like most cones, the revolving cone buries itself in sand during the day but comes out at night to hunt.
- Some cones actually catch fish and consume them whole.

Revolving cone

Conus circumactus

Some cone shells have a spiral sculpture, like this revolving cone. The shell is bright orange with two white bands. The spire is white with dark markings. You can very easily feel the raised bumps that run in spirals around the body whorl.

Wonder shell
Thatcheria mirabilis

The wonder shell belongs to a very large group of shells called the turrids. Although they are not cone-shaped, they are close relatives of the cone shells. The wonder shell has an amazing shape and cannot be confused with any other shell.

Habitat: Marine

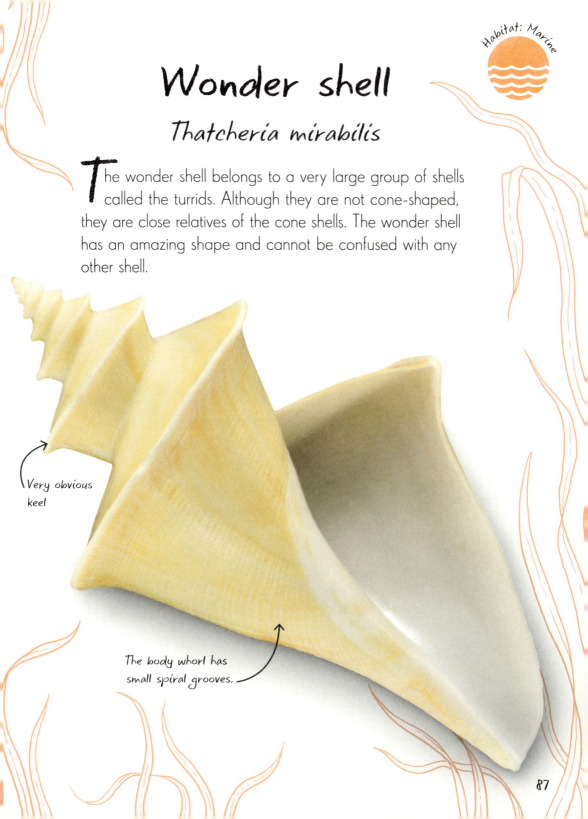

Very obvious keel

The body whorl has small spiral grooves.

87

Habitat: Marine

Blushing auger

Myurella russoi

The auger shells are all long and thin, and the animals bury themselves in sand during the day. They have more whorls in their shells than any other group of gastropods. The blushing auger lives in deep water and gets its name from its reddish-brown color.

Notes

• This blushing auger has 21 whorls, but some other types can have as many as 56!

• If you see a thin "trail" winding about in the sand under shallow water, it might be the trail left by an auger shell.

Strong axial ribs

Fine spiral sculpture in between the ribs

Habitat: Marine

Fine axial grooves on the smallest whorls only

This spiral alternates between brown dashes and white dashes.

Perspective sundial

Architectonica perspectiva

Sundial shells are almost perfectly round and from the side have a shape like a low dome. They have regular markings going around a spiral, which look like the marks on a clock or a sundial. Sometimes they are called the "winding staircase shells."

The opening at the base is called the "umbilicus," with a spiral of brown and white spots.

Habitat: Marine

The soft parts of the animal in this shell appear to float around in the water.

Red-lined bubble

Bullina lineata

Bubble shells tend to be thin, and the shell seems too small for the animal's body. Some do not have a shell at all (sea slugs). The red-lined bubble shell has an animal that is delicate and almost see-through. The shell's intricate pattern of red lines might remind you of icing on a cake.

Spiral grooves

Crenulated lip

Unbound bubble

Akera soluta

The shell of this very delicate mollusk is barely large enough for the animal to get inside! It is more like an internal shell that the animal rolls itself around. The coiling of the shell is completely open. With its lightweight shell, the unbound bubble is a very good swimmer.

Habitat: Marine

Notes

- Sometimes these shells are called "sea hares."
- They can be found in the Indian Ocean and western Pacific Ocean, including New Zealand.

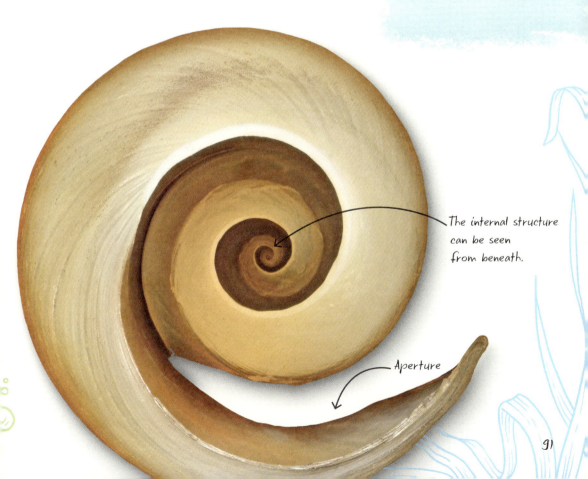

The internal structure can be seen from beneath.

Aperture

Is it a shell?

This book is about mollusk shells. You might come across other things in the sea that look like shells—but they are not from a mollusk. Perhaps you have seen some of these on the seashore.

Crab carapace

Crabs, shrimps, and lobsters belong to a large group called crustaceans, which are different from mollusks. Most crabs have a hard exoskeleton called a "carapace," and you might see crab carapaces on the beach. This one is from a red-spotted shame-faced crab (*Calappa rubroguttata*).

This strawberry hermit crab (*Coenobita perlatus*) has chosen a turban shell to live in.

Hermit crab

Is this a mollusk? Yes and no! The shell is the exoskeleton of a mollusk that has died. It's been taken over by a crab—a crustacean—that doesn't have an upper shell of its own. We call them hermit crabs, and they "borrow" mollusk shells for their own protection. They carry the shell around with them and can walk out of it at any time.

Sea urchin test

Sea urchins are not mollusks. Their hard exoskeleton is called a "test." This one is the exquisite sea urchin (*Coelopleurus exquisitus*). Notice how the pattern repeats five times as you go around. All sea urchins are like this—they have five-fold symmetry.

Repeated pattern

Brachiopod shell

A hole in the shell allows the pedicle to pass through.

The brachiopods are a large group of sea creatures that can easily be mistaken for bivalve mollusks. But the soft parts of the animal are very different from those of a mollusk. Most brachiopods have a stalk, called a "pedicle," to attach themselves to the seabed. This is a type of brachiopod called the bloodstained lamp shell (*Frenulina sanguinolenta*).

Habitat: Fresh water

Decorated lake snail

Margarya melanioides

Some gastropods live in rivers and lakes instead of in the sea. They are adapted to survive in fresh water. The decorated lake snail lives in certain Chinese lakes, where it used to be very common indeed. It has an operculum and a greenish or brownish periostracum.

Short projections around the body whorl

There are five or six spiral cords on the base.

Notes

• The baby snails grow inside eggs and are released from the mother only when they are ready to hatch.

• This snail likes to live in the muddy sand of lakes that are quite shallow.

94

Habitat: Fresh water

Spines on the shoulder

Spiral cords on the body whorl

Spiny freshwater snail
Tiphobia horei

No other freshwater snail is as spiny as this one. It lives only in Lake Tanganyika, in eastern Africa. About 65 different freshwater snails live in Lake Tanganyika and nowhere else in the world. The spiny freshwater snail has a very delicate lip that breaks easily.

Long, tapering siphonal canal

Habitat: Land

Mrs. De Burgh's tropid snail

Tropidophora deburghiae

Gastropods that live on land are called terrestrial gastropods, or "land snails." Seashells "breathe" with their gills (like fish), and Mrs. De Burgh's tropid snail also has gills, but not all land snails do. There are many beautiful types of tropid snails, mostly living in Madagascar.

Very strong carina

Thick operculum

Red lip

Habitat: Land

Aperture appears to be on the left

Body whorl twists backward and upward

Notes

• Although the aperture appears on the left, this snail is not sinistral. It just looks strange because the aperture faces backward!

• The aperture is round, which is typical of a land snail that has an operculum.

Little miracle snail

Plectostoma mirabile

This bizarre little snail lives on the walls of caves in Borneo, Southeast Asia. Caves are usually cool and damp, so in a hot country, they're a good place for a land snail to live. The little miracle snail seems to coil normally, apart from its spectacular body whorl.

Habitat: Land

Protoconch

The spines on this shell may give the animal some protection from predators.

Star-shaped lip

The hedgehog snail from hell

Blaesospira echinus infiernalis

With spines like a hedgehog, this fragile snail lives on limestone rock, up on steep mountains on the island of Cuba. The shell is uncoiled, except for the protoconch. The animal can clamp its aperture down against a rock and stay in place. It will do this to avoid drying out in dry weather.

The snowflake snail
Meganipha rhecta

Habitat: Land

The snowflake snail has many delicate varices, or old lips, that make it look like a magnified snowflake. It lives in a special habitat called a "cloud forest," where moist air keeps everything damp. Because it lives deep in the jungle, hardly anyone ever sees this beautiful snail.

Smooth protoconch, with no varices

Varices can be seen through the other side

Notes

- The varices will crumble to pieces when touched, however gentle you try to be.
- Sometimes it's called the "brittle snowflake snail," because the varices are so easy to break.

Habitat: Land

Apex can be white or pink

"Cloudy" blue band

Liguus tree snail

Liguus fasciatus

The Liguus tree snails are found in southern Florida, Cuba, and Hispaniola, and their colors and patterns vary enormously. Often, snails living in one small area will look quite different from their neighbors living in another group of trees. No Liguus shells have an operculum.

Notes

- The Liguus has lungs, not gills, for breathing.
- More than 80 different color forms of this snail have been given their own names.
- The typical size of the snail is 2 in (50 mm).

Habitat: Land

Brown band at the joint between the whorls

Final part of body whorl twists upward

Up-mouth snail
Anostoma carinatum

This strange-looking snail seems to have its mouth facing upward! The mouth is restricted by folds that look like little "teeth," which stop predators (birds and lizards) from eating the animal inside. The up-mouth snail lives in the Amazon rainforest, which is home to many exotic snails.

This shell has strong folds on the columella and the outer lip.

Habitat: Land

Pinched door snail
Grandinenia mirifica

The door snails have a club-shaped shell. Most door snails coil in the opposite direction to almost all the shells we've seen so far—if you look carefully at the spire, you can see that it coils to the left. Left-handed (sinistral) coiling is less unusual in land snails than in marine gastropods.

The biggest whorl is not usually the body whorl.

Notes

• When they're alive, door snails have a "flap" or "door" in their aperture, which has a similar purpose to an operculum.

• The door snails are the largest group of land snails—there are more than 1,300 different types!

The body whorl is "pinched" just before the aperture.

Habitat: Land

Green-banded snail
Eurystyla viridis

This green-banded snail has an outer skin on its shell called the "cuticle." It's not the same as periostracum. Most of the snail's color is contained in the cuticle. This snail lives only on the small island of Nosy Boraha, off the coast of Madagascar.

Rounded protoconch

Some cuticle has been rubbed off from this area.

This snail has its eyes on the ends of two stalks.

Habitat: Land

A crack has appeared across the body whorl.

This is the lip, now broken into two.

The shell has split apart at the umbilicus.

Exploding snail
Powelliphanta lignaria

Something rather strange happens to this shell after the animal has died. It has a very thick, hard periostracum, which gradually dries out. After some time, the tension in the periostracum causes the shell to "explode!" It happens in slow motion, taking many months. Only small pieces will remain.

Habitat: Land

Yellow-banded mirror snail

Amphidromus smithii

It's less common to see gastropods that have left-handed coiling, with their apertures on the left. The mirror snails are very unusual—their shells can coil either way! This yellow-banded mirror snail coils to the left and can be found in tropical forests.

Yellow spiral band

Notes

- The adult shell shown here has a lip that is curled back, or reflected. A young shell has just a thin lip that doesn't curl back.

- Indonesia has the biggest variety of mirror snails—often one type lives on a single small island and nowhere else.

Aperture is on the left

Shells for decoration

Artists and craftspeople are inspired by shells. They depict them in their designs, and they incorporate the shells themselves into their creations.

Jewelry

Shells have been used to make jewelry throughout human history, and they are still used today. A single shell can be made into a brooch or an earring. Sometimes it is silver or gold-plated. Shells are often strung together into headbands, bracelets, or elaborate necklaces.

This necklace is made from ringed cowries (*Monetaria annulus*).

The nacre on the inside of the shells gives a metallic effect.

Masks

As well as adorning their bodies with shell jewelry, people make face masks out of shells. This can be very creative! It's something that people have done since the Stone Age, when people would carve holes in shells for their eyes and mouth. More modern masks are pieced together with lots of different types of shells for a striking image.

This cameo was carved into an emperor helmet shell (*Cassis madagascariensis*).

Cameos

A skilled craftsperson can carve a picture into the back of a large shell. This is called a cameo. A cameo can be worn as a brooch, or it can remain as part of the whole shell. This example shows a woman driving a chariot.

Home decoration

The nacre, or mother-of-pearl, from abalones is often used for decorating objects and even furniture. It has a colorful shine to it, which changes when you look at it from different angles. This exquisite pitcher from India is completely covered with thin slices of abalone shell.

The light provides a rainbow sheen to the nacre.

The pattern of ribs resembles a scallop shell.

Architecture

Even architects—people who design buildings—have been inspired by shells. There are entire buildings that seem to be coiled like a gastropod shell. A half-dome in the shape of a scallop is a common feature in buildings from Roman times onward.

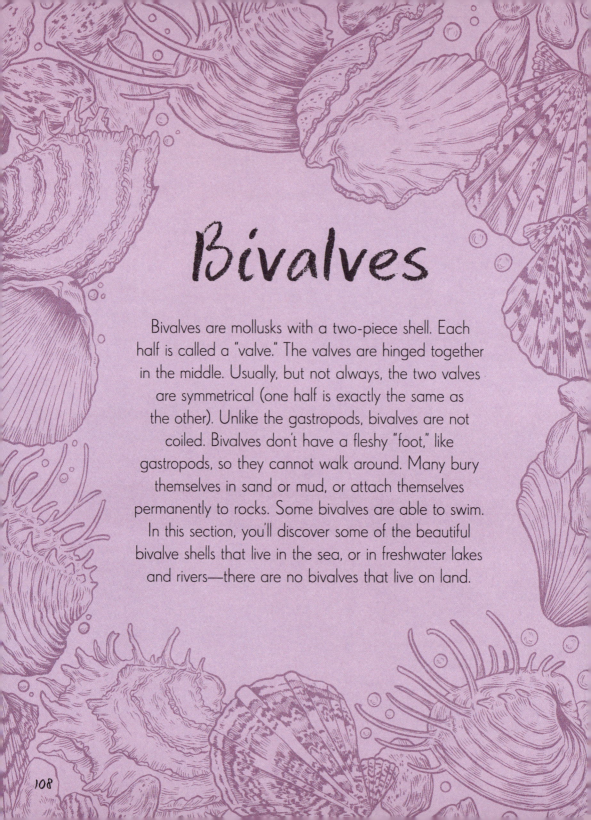

Bivalves

Bivalves are mollusks with a two-piece shell. Each half is called a "valve." The valves are hinged together in the middle. Usually, but not always, the two valves are symmetrical (one half is exactly the same as the other). Unlike the gastropods, bivalves are not coiled. Bivalves don't have a fleshy "foot," like gastropods, so they cannot walk around. Many bury themselves in sand or mud, or attach themselves permanently to rocks. Some bivalves are able to swim. In this section, you'll discover some of the beautiful bivalve shells that live in the sea, or in freshwater lakes and rivers—there are no bivalves that live on land.

Habitat: Marine

Right valve

Umbo

Left valve

Crowned cockle

Vepricardium coronatum

Cockles bury themselves in sand or mud, and their empty shells often wash up on beaches. Most have strong ribs that radiate out from the umbo. The umbo is the part of the shell that forms first and is closest to the hinge.

Notes

- The ribs of the crowned cockle are not smooth—they have very small spines.

- The ribs of each valve match up at their edge exactly and allow the shell to seal itself shut.

Habitat: Marine

Some ribs are so well developed that they look like spines.

Valves are joined by the ligament (stretchy material covering the hinge).

Wedding cake Venus

Bassina disjecta

Venus clams take the name of the Roman goddess of love because they are so beautiful. Their ribs are arranged in "concentric" rings, meaning they all have the same center. This bivalve lives in the sand or mud around southern Australia and Tasmania.

The ribs of this shell are frilly, like icing on a cake.

Habitat: Marine

Spine

Concentric ribs

Notes

• The spined Venus is a common shell but is rarely seen in its full and unbroken state.

• Some gastropods like to eat the spined Venus, drilling a hole in its shell and sucking out the animal.

Spined Venus

Hysteroconcha lupanaria

This spectacular shell has two rows of spines on each valve. The spines probably protect the soft parts of the animal when it emerges from the shell. The empty shell must be handled with great care, because the spines are very delicate.

Habitat: Marine

Beautiful sunset clam
Gari pulcherrima

The sunset clams are delicate bivalves that usually live in mud. The beautiful sunset clam has a very unusual sculpture—a combination of radial ridges and oblique (neither radial nor concentric) ridges. Often, the empty shells wash up on beaches, still attached together in a pair.

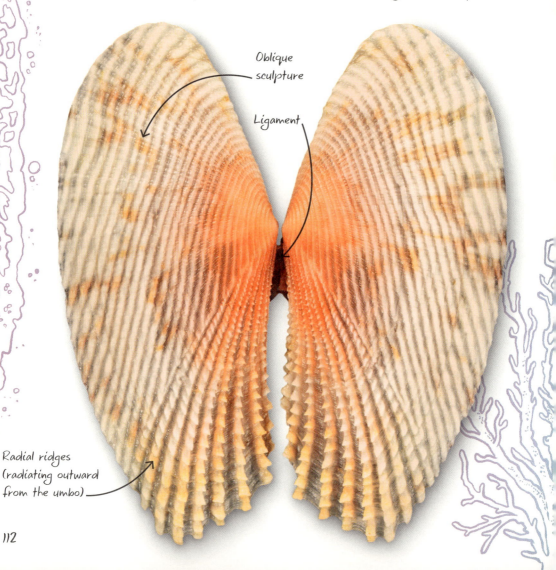

Oblique sculpture

Ligament

Radial ridges (radiating outward from the umbo)

Minor spine

"Spatulate" spine (shaped like a spatula)

Major spine

Habitat: Marine

Victoria thorny oyster

Spondylus victoriae

The thorny oysters are large, heavy shells that grow spines. The spines invite other animals to attach themselves, so when the mollusks are alive, these shells look very messy! The Victoria thorny oyster usually has spines that are longer than the main part of the shell.

Notes

- The thorny oysters are more closely related to scallops than to oysters, so perhaps we should call them "thorny scallops" instead!

- Sometimes, pearls grow on the inner surface of the shell.

Habitat: Marine

Somali scallop

Mirapecten cranmerorum

The scallops are a large group of colorful shells, shaped like fans. They live in all the world's seas, even beneath the ice around Antarctica. The Somali scallop lives in deep water off the east coast of Africa. It has only five very broad ribs.

Notes
- The Somali scallop can be red or orange, or a combination of both.
- Unlike most bivalves, scallops can swim, by flapping their valves together to create "jet propulsion."

Auricle (sometimes called the "ear")

Tubercle (a round swelling on a rib)

Diana's scallop

Semipallium dianae

Habitat: Marine

Often, there are several different color forms of a scallop. Diana's scallop can be purple, yellow, red, orange, or any combination of those colors. However, the umbo is always orange. When you look very closely, you can see that the shell's surface has a fine sculpture, which looks like a honeycomb.

Orange umbo

One auricle is much bigger than the other.

Each scallop has about 100 eyes, able to detect a predator.

115

Habitat: Marine

Hinge consisting of two ridges

Notes

• The interior and exterior of this shell look almost identical.

• These shells can be used in the place of window panes to construct windows, by gluing them into a wooden frame.

This is actually the inside of the shell.

Square window-pane clam

Placuna quadrangula

These shells are so thin that you can see right through many of them. So they are known as window-pane clams. They live in mud and are very fragile. Almost no other bivalves are square-shaped like this unusual shell.

Australian watering pot

Brechites australis

Habitat: Marine

Front end is open

Here is a bivalve that looks nothing like a bivalve! It appears to be a long tube, with one end open and the other end buried deep in the sand or gravel. Look closely at the side of the tube to see the young bivalve shell.

The typical length of the tube is 6.5 in (17 cm).

The lower end has many small holes, just like a watering pot!

Young shell attached to the side of the tube

Habitat: Fresh water

Elliptical African oyster
Etheria elliptica

Some freshwater lakes and rivers make splendid habitats for bivalves. These bivalves that are adapted to fresh water are often called "freshwater oysters," or "freshwater mussels." The elliptical African oyster is common in Africa's largest lake, Lake Victoria. The shape varies, and it can look very "untidy."

The inside is covered in "blisters" of mother-of-pearl, also known as nacre.

The two valves that form this shell are different shapes.

Pistolgrip
Tritogonia verrucosa

The river systems of the eastern US are home to about 300 different freshwater mussels, and many have unusually sculptured surfaces. This river mussel is called the "pistolgrip" because the rough surface feels like the handle of a pistol. It is a very thick and heavy shell.

Habitat: Fresh water

"Warty" surface with typically triangular bumps

Umbo

Notes

• The pistolgrip is endangered, like many American freshwater mussels. This is because of river pollution and human changes to the water systems (such as dams).

• You can tell males and females apart by their slightly different shapes; this is a female.

Color may be green, brown, or black

Other types of mollusks

Most mollusk shells that you'll see are either gastropods or bivalves. There are other groups of mollusks that might not look so familiar. The cephalopods include large animals with tentacles, such as octopuses, cuttlefishes, squids, and nautiluses. The chitons are flat, oval-shaped creatures with eight hard "plates." Tusk shells are long and thin and look like miniature elephant tusks. These groups look very different from one another—but they are all mollusks. In this section, you'll discover some of these other mollusk shells, which can be found in all the world's oceans.

Paper nautilus

Argonauta argo

Habitat: Marine

The paper nautilus is a type of octopus, quite different from the protected pearly nautilus because it doesn't actually live inside a "shell." Instead, the female has a paper-thin case to protect her eggs. She also uses the egg case as a flotation device to stay on the ocean's surface.

The case is as thin as a sheet of paper.

The case can be more than 8 in (20 cm) long.

The female's egg case can hold 40,000 eggs! Males have no case at all.

121

Habitat: Marine

Head end

Spectacular chiton

Mopalia spectabilis

Chitons have an exoskeleton made of eight hard "plates" that overlap, like armor. The eight plates are held together by a soft, fleshy band. Chitons cling tightly to rocks, but they can move around using a large muscular "foot" enclosed by the plates. Chiton is spoken with a hard "C," pronounced as "kai-tun."

The pustules on the plates are blue-green and red.

Rear end

Habitat: Marine

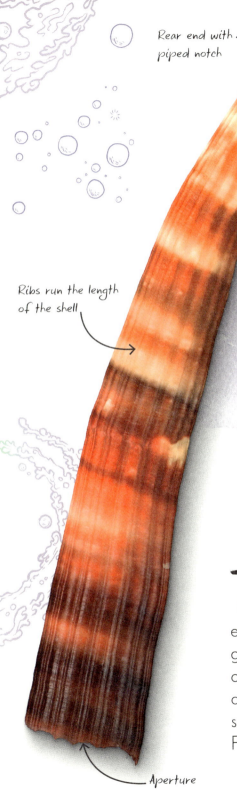

Rear end with piped notch

Ribs run the length of the shell

Aperture

Notes

- The Formosan tusk is usually covered in alternating bands of red and cream.
- Tusk shells live buried in sand or mud, with the narrow rear end pointing upward.
- Tusk shells have been used to make necklaces for thousands of years.

Formosan tusk

Pictodentalium formosum

Tusk shells are mollusks with a single shell that is thin and narrower toward one end. The shell is curved, but it is not coiled like a gastropod shell. The rear end may have a notch, or a small "pipe," and the animal emerges at the aperture end. Many tusk shells are white, but some types are more colorful, such as this Formosan tusk.

Glossary

aperture
Opening at the front end of a gastropod shell

apex
Top of a gastropod's spire

auricle
Triangular structure near the
hinge of some bivalve shells

axial
Type of sculpture or pattern running
up and down the whorl of a gastropod,
rather than in a spiral

bivalve
Mollusk with a two-piece shell

body whorl
Final whorl of an adult gastropod shell

carina
Noticeable sharp ridge on a shell, also called a "keel"

cephalopod
Type of mollusk such as a nautilus,
squid, octopus, or cuttlefish

chiton
Mollusk with eight shelly plates
held together by a band of flesh

clam
Several different kinds of bivalves

columella
Central "pillar" of a gastropod shell,
seen to one side of the aperture

concentric sculpture
Ribs or ridges arranged in rings that
share the same center

cord
Spiral ridge around a gastropod shell

crenulated
Crinkled or wavy

denticles
Small, regular structures that look like teeth

dextral
Right-handed coiling of a gastropod shell,
meaning the aperture is on the right

exoskeleton
Hard skeleton that's on the outside
of an animal, such as the shell of a mollusk

fold
Feature on a shell that looks like a crease

foot
Large, fleshy mass that can protrude from the shell

fresh water
Water in a river or a lake, which is not salty

gastropod
Mollusk that has a one-piece shell, or a related
mollusk such as a slug

gills
Organs that most mollusks use to extract oxygen
from water or air

habitat
Type of environment that an animal or plant lives in

hinge
Edge of one half of a bivalve shell that
interlocks with the edge of its opposite half

land snail
Gastropod that lives on land, not in water

ligament
Elastic structure that joins two halves
of a bivalve shell

lime
Group of chemicals that make up most of
a mollusk shell

lip
Outer edge of a gastropod's aperture

mantle
Part of the living mollusk that creates the shell

mollusk
Soft-bodied, legless, and boneless animal, which often has a hard shell

nacre
Shiny inner surface of many shells, commonly known as mother-of-pearl

node
Knob on a shell's surface, larger than a pustule but smaller than a tubercle

oblique sculpture
Sculpture forming in straight lines that are neither concentric nor radial

operculum
Part of many gastropods that is used to close the aperture, like a trapdoor

parietal shield
Structure that joins the columella and covers part of the body whorl on some gastropods

periostracum
Type of "skin" on the outside of some shells

predator
Animal that kills other animals and eats them

protoconch
Youngest part of a shell

pustule
Small, round knob or bead on a shell, smaller than a node or a tubercle

range
Area of the world where a certain type of shell lives

radial sculpture
Sculpture in straight lines going outward from one central point

reflected lip
Gastropod lip that curls back on itself

rib
Ridge on a shell's surface, which can be axial or spiraling

sinistral
Left-handed coiling of a gastropod shell, meaning the aperture is on the left

siphonal canal
Channel or tube leading from an aquatic gastropod's aperture, where water travels in and out

snail
Any gastropod that has a shell (including those in the sea)

spine
Thin, outward projection from the surface of a shell

spire
Coiled part of a gastropod shell, excluding the body whorl

tubercle
Large, rounded knob, larger than a node or a pustule

tusk shell
Mollusk with a long, thin, narrowing shell that is not coiled

umbilicus
Opening at the base of many gastropods

umbo
Part of a bivalve shell's valve that forms first, closest to the hinge

valve
One half of a bivalve shell, or one plate of a chiton

varix
Thickening left over from a previous lip of a gastropod shell

veliger
Young larva of some mollusks

ventrum
Side of a gastropod shell that has the aperture

waste canal
Channel or tube at the top end of the aperture of some gastropods, for expelling waste

whorl
One single turn (coil) of a gastropod shell

Index

A

abalones 17, 107
annularid land snail 6
auger shells 88
auricles 114, 115
Australian pheasant shell 13
Australian watering pot 117

B

Babylon shells 70
beautiful sunset clam 112
bivalves 7, 26, 27, 57, 108–119
bleeding tooth 16
blistered egg cowrie 34
bloodstained lamp shell 93
blushing auger 88
brachiopods 93
brackish water habitat 20
breathing 17, 18, 96, 100
bubble shells 90–91
bull conch 23
Burnett's thorn-mouth 64
butterfly murex 62

C

callus 81
cameos 107
camouflage 26
Cape cowrie 32
carapaces 92
carrier shells 26–27
cephalopods 57, 120, 121
checkerboard goblet shell 47
Chinese carrier shell 27
chitons 120, 122
Clover's volute 74
club murex 61
cockles 109
coiling 10, 11, 50, 97, 102, 105
columella 16, 19, 32, 35, 41, 47, 54,
   55, 60, 61, 67, 71, 72, 77, 80, 81, 101
common wentletrap 45
conchs 22–24, 38, 54, 56
cone shells 82–86, 87
coral shells 65
corals/coral reefs 8, 33, 34, 56, 65
cords 36, 48, 49, 84, 94, 95
cowrie shells 28–34, 39, 106
crabs 92

cracked miter 79
crowned cockle 109
crustaceans 92
cuticle 103

D

decorated lake snail 94
deep sea 9, 46
denticles 37, 41, 42, 43, 47, 52,
   61, 62, 77
dextral shells 50
Diana's scallop 115
distortion shells 42
dolphin shells 15
door snails 102
dove shells 52

E

egg cases 121
egg cowries 33–34
elliptical African oyster 118
emerald green tree snail 57
Emperor's egg cowrie 33
exoskeletons 6, 92, 93, 122
exploding snail 104

F

false olive 81
false trumpet shell 66
feeding 7, 27, 35, 44, 59, 64, 81
festive mini-spindle 55
festive volute 72
fingered spider conch 24
flaked wentletrap 7
flame shell 7
Formosan tusk 123
freshwater bivalves 57, 118–119
freshwater gastropods 94–95
frog shells 43

G

Galápagos helmet shell 37
gastropods 10–91, 94–105
giant clams 56
gills 96, 100
girdled star shell 14
Glory of the Atlantic 84
Glory of Bengal 85
Glory of India 85

Glory of the Ocean 84
Glory of the Seas 84
goblet shells 47
golden cowrie 29
great spotted cowrie 30
green-banded snail 103

H

harp shells 76
hedgehog snail from hell 98
hefty screw shell 21
helmet shells 37, 107
hermit crabs 92
Hessler's hairy vent shell 46
hinges 7, 16, 109, 110, 116
horn shells 19
horse conchs 54
hunting 35, 64, 72, 83, 86

I

Indian chank 39
iridescence 12

J

Japanese corded whelk 48
jewelry 106
Johnson's volute 6

K

keels (carinas) 66, 68, 87, 96
keyhole limpets 18
knobbed triton 39
Kuiper's ribbed miter 69

L

lakes 9, 10, 94–95, 108, 118
Lamarck's frog shell 43
land snails 6, 9, 10, 56–57, 96–105
law, shells and the 2, 56–57
lightning whelk 50
Liguus tree snail 100
lime 6, 9, 13
limpets 18
lined spindle shell 51
little miracle snail 97
long-spined dolphin shell 15
love harp 76

M

Maltese cross cowrie 31

126

mantle 30, 34, 35, 36, 77
margin shells 77
marine habitat 11–37, 40–55, 58–91, 109–117, 121–123
miraculous soft-cap 25
mirror shells 105
miter shells 79
mollusks 6–7, 10, 108, 120
moon shells 35
Moriori abalone 17
movement 23, 41, 108, 114, 122
Mrs. De Burgh's tropid snail 96
Mrs. Roadnight's volute 75
mud creepers 20
mud snails 53
murex shells 58–65
musical shells 37, 38–39
mussels, freshwater 118–119

N

nacre (mother-of-pearl) 17, 106, 107, 118
nautiluses 57, 120, 121
Neapolitan triton 41
nerites 16
niso shells 44
nocturnal activity 34, 79, 80
nutmeg shells 78

O

O'ahu tree snail 56
olive shells 80–81
onion shell 71
operculum 11, 13, 14, 15, 16, 23, 44, 48, 74, 81, 94, 96, 97
orchid murex 59
ormers 17
oysters, freshwater 118

P

Pacific triton 38
pagoda shells 68
pale carrier shell 26
paper nautilus 121
parasitic shells 44, 45
parietal shield 42, 67
Pavlova's typhis 63
pearly nautilus 57
periostracum 25, 40, 41, 42, 46, 94, 104
Persian horse conch 54
perspective sundial 89
Peruvian conch 38
pheasant shells 13
pimpled mud shell 53

pinched door snail 102
pistolgrip 119
Polymita snails 57
Ponsonby's volute 73
pot-bellied fig 36
prince's horn shell 19
protected shells 56–57
protoconch 52, 53, 68, 98, 99, 103

Q

queen conch 56
queen margin shell 77

R

red-lined bubble 90
revolving cone 86
ribbed miters 69, 79
ringed top 11
rivers and streams 9, 10, 94, 108, 119
Robinson's distortion shell 42
rose-branch murex 58
rough carrier shell 26

S

scallops 113, 114–115
screw shells 21
sea hares 91
sea urchins 93
sinistral shells 50, 97, 102, 105
siphonal canal 19, 22, 24, 49, 50, 51, 54, 59, 60, 63, 68, 82, 86, 95
slugs 10
snowflake snail 99
soft-cap shells 25
Somali scallop 114
South African keyhole limpet 18
spectacular chiton 122
spider conchs 24
spiky pagoda shell 68
spined Venus 111
spines 6, 14, 15, 23, 27, 58, 60, 65, 67, 68, 78, 95, 98, 109, 111, 113
spiny carrier shell 27
spiny coral shell 65
spiny freshwater snail 95
spiral Babylon 70
splendid dove shell 52
splendid niso 44
spotted top 12
square window-pane clam 116
star shells 14
stings, venomous 2, 83
strawberry clam 56

stromboid notch 22–24
sundial shells 89

T

tent olive 80
tests 93
textile cone 83
thorn-mouths 64
thorny oysters 113
top shells 11, 12
Torr's whelk 49
tritons 38, 39, 40–41, 42
tubercles 43, 54, 114
turrids 87
tusk shells 120, 123
typhis shells 63

U

umbilicus 89, 104
umbo 109, 112, 115
unbound bubble 91
uncoiled nutmeg 78
up-mouth snail 101

V

varices 59, 61, 62, 64, 99
vase shells 55, 66, 67
veliger 41
ventrum 29
Venus clams 110–111
Venus comb 60
victor cone 82
Victoria thorny oyster 113
violet moon shell 35
volutes 6, 72–75
vomer conch 22

W

wedding cake Venus 110
wentletraps 7, 45
West African carrier shell 27
West African mud creeper 20
whelks 48–50, 55
whorls 10, 21, 37, 45, 78, 88, 102
window-pane clams 116
winged triton 40
wonder shell 87

Y

yellow-banded mirror snail 105

Z

Zanzibar vase 67
zigzag cowrie 28

Editors Abi Maxwell, Srijani Ganguly
Senior Art Editor Kanika Kalra
Project Art Editor Bhagyashree Nayak
Art Editor Nishtha Gupta
US Senior Editor Jennette ElNaggar
DTP Designers Anita Yadav, Syed Md Farhan
Picture Researcher Ridhima Sikka
Senior Jacket Designer Rashika Kachroo
Managing Editors Gemma Farr, Roohi Sehgal
Managing Art Editors Elle Ward, Ivy Sengupta
Senior Production Editor Nikoleta Parasaki
Production Controller John Casey
Delhi Creative Head Malavika Talukder
Art Director Mabel Chan

Editorial Consultant Phil Hunt

First American Edition, 2025
Published in the United States by DK Publishing,
a division of Penguin Random House LLC
1745 Broadway, 20th Floor, New York, NY 10019

About the author:
Dr. Simon P. Aiken is a prominent author and researcher of shells, as well as a natural history photographer. DK would like to especially thank Simon for allowing us access to his extensive photo library for this project.

DK would like to thank:
Polly Goodman for proofreading; Helen Peters for the index; Daniel Long for the feature illustrations; Angela Rizza for the pattern and cover illustrations; Mohd. Zishan for additional illustrations.

From the author:
A number of the photographs in this book are of shells from the collection of Carl Ruscoe and Craig Ruscoe, Lancashire, UK. I'd like to thank the Ruscoes for allowing access to their magnificent shell collection. I also thank Jonathan Welsh for the loan of several shells.

Copyright © 2025 Dorling Kindersley Limited
25 26 27 28 29 10 9 8 7 6 5 4 3 2 1
001–345732–Jun/2025

All rights reserved.
Without limiting the rights under the copyright reserved above, no part of this publication may be reproduced, stored in or introduced into a retrieval system, or transmitted, in any form, or by any means (electronic, mechanical, photocopying, recording, or otherwise), without the prior written permission of the copyright owner.
Published in Great Britain by Dorling Kindersley Limited

A catalog record for this book
is available from the Library of Congress.
ISBN 978-0-5939-6541-2

Printed and bound in China

www.dk.com

This book was made with Forest Stewardship Council™ certified paper—one small step in DK's commitment to a sustainable future.
Learn more at www.dk.com/uk/information/sustainability

The publisher would like to thank the following for their kind permission to reproduce their photographs. (Key: a-above; b-below/bottom; c-center; f-far; l-left; r-right; t-top)

2 Alamy Stock Photo: ChasingSunsets / Stockimo (t). **7 naturepl.com:** Alex Mustard (br). **8 Alamy Stock Photo:** Cavan Images (b). **Dreamstime.com:** Vitalii Hryshko (cla). **9 Alamy Stock Photo:** geogphotos (cl). **Ocean Exploration Trust:** Ocean Exploration Trust / NOAA (tr). **38 Alamy Stock Photo:** imageBROKER GmbH & Co. KG n / Norbert Probst (br); Carlos Mora (crb). **39 Alamy Stock Photo:** MAXPPP / Frederic Charmeux (tr). **Dreamstime.com:** Mohamed Abdelrazek (br). **The Metropolitan Museum of Art:** Purchase, The Barrington Foundation Inc. Gift, 1986 (cl). **57 naturepl.com:** Bruno D'Amicis (tr). **92 Getty Images:** 500px / Jean Philippe Barbe (bl). **106 Creation of Caroline Perrin:** (br). **Shutterstock.com:** Gaia Conventi (cr). **107 Alamy Stock Photo:** Ivan Vdovin. © The Trustees of the British Museum. All rights reserved: (cr). **Chez Pluie Provence:** Chez Pluie Provence (tl)

All other images by Dr. Simon P. Aiken

128